NAME-DROPPING

The Life and Lies of Alan King

ALAN KING
WITH CHRIS CHASE

A TOUCHSTONE BOOK
Published by Simon & Schuster

TOUCHSTONE
Rockefeller Center
1230 Avenue of the Americas
New York, NY 10020

First Touchstone Edition 1997

TOUCHSTONE and colophon are trademarks of Simon & Schuster Inc.

Designed by Brooke Zimmer

Manufactured in the United States of America

1 3 5 7 9 10 8 6 4 2

Library of Congress Cataloging-in-Publication Data
King, Alan, date.
Name-dropping : the life and lies of Alan King / Alan King with Chris
Chase.
p. cm.
Includes index.
1. King, Alan. 2. Comedians—United States—Biography.
3. Actors—United States—Biography. 1. Chase, Chris. 11. Title.
PN2287.K6687A3 1996
792.7'028'092—dc20
[B] 96-626
CIP
ISBN 0-684-80384-4
0-684-83278-X (pbk)

TO MY FAMILY

Robert, Andrew and Judy,
Steve and Elainie

Teddy, Billy, Annika, Madeleine,
and Brendon Jamie

and to
Jeanette, my lover and best friend

Acknowledgments

They have touched my life.

Harry Adler, Sid Gathrid, Jack London, Jilly Rizzo, Carol Burnett, Billy Eckstine, Buddy Rich, Ed Sullivan, Sidney Korchak, Florence and Murray White, Garry Moore, Walter Hyman, Charles Allen, Elie Wiesel, Jackie Robinson, Sherry and Buddy Hackett, Whoopi Goldberg, Bruce Charet, Louise Cooper, Charlie Rapp, Rabbi Wolfe, Harry Crane, Lucho Gatica, Lola and Nat Finkelstein, Fran Shoten, Steve Smith, Nancy and Zubin Mehta, Cliff Perlman, Vitas Gerulaitis, Sheila and Gordon Macrae, Harry Richman, Mimi Sheraton, Lisa Traina, Itzhak Perlman, Dr. Norman Rosenthal, Dr. Keith Heller, Dr. James and Dolores Scuibba, Kay and Eddy Ray, Alice and Lou Weiss, Margo and Irwin Winkler, Sue and Herman Merinoff, Simone and William Levitt, Renee and Steve Levy, Anthony Newley, Adele and Robert Frankel, the Dorman Family, Mary and Peter Stone, Dave Flaim, Maurice Chevalier, Joyce and George Wein, Paddy Chayefsky, Bob Fosse, Gabe Sumner, John Schreiber, Josephine Baker, Evaristo De Loureiro, Anita and Jack Pollack, Jack Wasserman, Herb Sargent, Daniel Kossow, Danny Welkes, Owen Laster, Pat and Fred Stolle, Arthur Miller, Phil Silvers, Lee Salomon, Lee Solters, The "Count," The "Duke," Woody, Benny, and Artie.

I hope that those of the above who are still living will be so thrilled to be mentioned that they'll all go out and buy several copies.

Contents

NAME-
DROPPING

PROLOGUE

YOU'RE BORN, YOU LIVE, YOU DIE. And along the way, in the twilight, so to speak, if you want to pick up a few extra dollars, you write your memoirs.

But this is not going to be a tell-all book. My few dark secrets I'm taking to my grave. I've had one wife since I was nineteen, our kids have turned out well; in retrospect, any problems I had don't seem that important anymore.

Also, this book is not going to be heavy drama—I don't want Robert De Niro playing my life—it's about where I've come from and what I've done in a career that's been going on for more than fifty years. And it's about friends famous and not so famous, and funny things that have happened to me and them.

It won't be chronological, either—you'll need a scorecard—and there's going to be a lot of shtick, because that's what a good part of my life was about.

Am I going to drop names? Yes. Whenever possible. Once, when I was running a big company, I called in all the people who were working for me and explained what I expected of them. "The one thing I don't want anybody to do, the one thing I will not tolerate, is name-dropping. It's bad. Marlon Brando told me that."

So I'll tell stories about Marlon Brando and Frank Sinatra and Charlie Chaplin and Judy Garland and Billy Crystal. (I played Billy's father in *Memories of Me*, and I always say he's become like one of my sons—he never calls, he never sends money.) And some of these stories may be lies. But I've told them for so long that I don't remember what is true and what is not true. The fact that a lot of people in this book are dead makes it easier for me to talk about them.

My mother and father were immigrants. They came from the old country, down in the bottom of the ship like cattle. That's why it's called steerage. On the other hand, I live in a mansion built for Oscar Hammerstein II. I still think that one morning I'm going to wake up, and there are going to be lights sweeping the property, and a guy with a bullhorn on the lawn, and he's going to yell, "Okay, Alan, the place is surrounded, leave all your possessions, just come out."

I'll be exposed, finally, because it's a joke, what I do—what *all* performers do. (If nobody wanted to pay us, we'd be doing it for nothing.) But so far, I've been lucky.

I remember taking my mother to see the musical *Fiddler on the Roof*. My mother was born in a village very like Anatevka, the setting for *Fiddler*. And when the show was over, and we were back out on the street, I said, "Ma, how did you enjoy it? Did it bring back memories?" "It was wonderful," she said. "Only I don't remember so much singing and dancing."

In this book, I'm not going to remember the bad stuff, I'm only going to remember the singing and dancing.

1 ∽ That's My Pop

my father moved through dooms of feel;
his anger was as right as rain
his pity was as green as grain

—E. E. CUMMINGS

As a young man, my father, Bernard Kniberg, traveled. He and one of his brothers walked across the face of Eastern Europe, and then my father got on a boat and sailed to America. If you'll pardon the cliché, the storm clouds of World War I were already gathering over Europe, and my father came here, and he didn't speak a word of English.

He was in this country sixteen weeks when he was drafted. And the same ship that he'd come over on was now a troop transport, and he was sent back to the country he'd just escaped from on the very boat he'd just escaped in. And the only language he spoke was the language of his enemy. He was a little confused.

On his return from the war, he met my mother, Minnie Solomon. He was already worldly, she was not. Also European born, she came from a very large family with fourteen children. She set the table, went to school, helped her mother clean the fish. Her father was a rabbi, her brothers were housepainters, hardworking people, good, honest people who still had the mentality of a small town. They lived a kind of shtetl existence; the world ended at the corner of their block.

But my father, my father—I have pictures of him when he was a young man, before the Depression. You see him in a bowler hat, a derby; he was a dude. He was also an intellectual and a dreamer. My mother's family, so conservative, so provincial, considered him a half-baked radical, an outsider who couldn't hold a job. They always thought their Minnie should have done better.

Maybe she could have done better, but she couldn't have done longer. My father died at ninety-six, my mother at ninety-one; they were together seventy years, and all that time, they never talked to each other, they only talked *across* each other. My mother would say, "Tell your father dinner's ready." I'd say, "He's sitting right here, why don't *you* tell him?" and she'd say, "I wouldn't give him the satisfaction."

Minnie and Bernie were Burns and Allen with a Jewish accent; they were *The Honeymooners*, always bickering, and they never knew how funny they were. When they were old and living in Florida, my sister used to phone me to complain about them. My sister lived three blocks from my parents. She didn't *want* to live three blocks from my parents, but I supported her, so she lived where I told her to live. And this one time she called me up and said, "You've gotta do something, they're fighting like cats and dogs."

I flew down there, walked into their living room, and they were sitting with their backs to each other. I said, "What's going on?" My mother spoke. "He plays the television too loud." "I'm deaf," says my father. "I *gotta* play the television loud." "But what about the neighbors?" says my mother. My father says, "Fuck the neighbors."

My mother starts yelling, "Look how he talks, look how he talks, whoever heard language like that?"

Now I'm standing there hysterical, and the minute she sees me laughing, she wheels on me. "Sure," she says, "you always take his side." Then, to my father: "You shut up, Bernie, don't ever use language like that again!"

There's a little terrace off their apartment, and my father gets up, opens the door to the terrace, walks out, and shouts to the world at large, "Fuck the neighbors!" Kind of showing me, you know, nobody fools with Bernie Kniberg. It was like a scene from the movie *Network*.

But their fighting never interfered with their concern and love for the children. There were eight of us, and I was the youngest, vying for attention. I was also Bernie and Minnie's only natural son, and I had one blood sister, Anita; all the others were my cousins, orphaned nieces and nephews of my mother's whom my parents took in. My parents were very giving people—they had nothing, but my mother used to cook for the neighbors, she could take a pound of chopped meat and stretch it so it fed twelve people. And this was before Hamburger Helper.

Sometimes in my act I talk about my beginnings. "I was born on the twenty-fifth of December," I say. "I know there was another very important Jew born on the same day. I wasn't born in a manger, I was born on the Lower East Side, which is as close as you can get to a manger."

I was named Irwin Alan Kniberg, and when I was very small, we moved to what I liked to call waterfront property (near the East River) in Williamsburg, Brooklyn, another ghetto. We lived on the fifth floor of a tenement—no elevator, it was a walk-up—between the Bond bread factory and the Schaefer brewery.

My father worked for the ILGWU, the garment workers' union headed by David Dubinsky. Dubinsky was a giant, and my father revered him. (Nobody ever said David Dubinsky, it was just one word, Dubinsky, like Sinatra or Liza or Lena or Toscanini.) One day my old man came home after having taken part in a strike, and he had a bloody towel wrapped around his head. My mother started screaming, "*Oy, gevalt*, whaddaya doin', Bernie? Why do you do this?" And my father gestured toward us—all the kids, who were playing in the hall— and he said, "So they won't have to."

That scene is embedded in my head. My father, like most of the other immigrant Jews in America, became a New Deal Democrat, and I've retained most of his ideas. I'm a knee-jerk limousine liberal, even though I've been rich much longer than I was poor. But the poor years you never forget. When you come from poverty, you go one of two ways; either you become a spender, like money doesn't mean anything (which I have a tendency to do; it's been said that if I drop a quarter on the floor and the bellhop picks it up, I give him a dollar tip), or you become terribly frugal. Because you think maybe they're going to take the money away.

Roosevelt's New Deal didn't help my father much; the American dream didn't pan out for him. During the Depression he must have had forty-two different jobs. He worked at a sewing machine, he sold housedresses on a pole in the marketplace (the housedresses were called Hooverettes, in honor of the president whom Roosevelt had driven from the White House), and when he didn't have work, we went on relief. To this day, relief sounds better to me than welfare—it sounds temporary, where welfare sounds like it's a permanent way of life.

In the relief days, the social workers used to come to your house to find out who was trying to cheat the system. They always visited Jewish houses late on Friday afternoons, before the Sabbath. And one social worker said to my mother, "I like to come here, because everyone else thinks they have to make their house look dirty, so I shouldn't think they're doing too good and they don't deserve help." But my mother was above that, our place had to be clean.

For my father, the humiliation of not being able to support us, of having to turn in tickets for day-old bread (we'd stand in line outside the Dugan bakery, and if there was a stale or damaged package of bread, we'd get it), was compounded by the fact that he had to give up his home and move us all in with my mother's father.

If my mother's family had contempt for my father's fecklessness, he detested them right back, especially because he had to endure their charity. My mother's mother died young, in 1933—I was six, and all I remember about Fannie Solomon is that she was a big blonde; my grandfather always liked big fair-haired women. After that, my mother became the matriarch. She brought up her sisters and brothers and took care of my grandfather, plus her own family.

Not that my grandfather couldn't take care of himself. A Russian, he had the soul of a cossack and he was strong as a bull. Besides being a rabbi, he was a janitor; he used to haul garbage cans, and in those days they were metal cans filled with ashes. He scared everybody. If a neighborhood kid didn't want to eat, his mother would say, "We're gonna call Rabbi Solomon." It was like threatening to call the bogeyman.

Rabbi Harry Solomon. He was a piece of work. When he landed at Ellis Island, his family name was Dworetsky. He had thirteen siblings named Dworetsky, and they had all preceded him to America. In those days, it was the oldest brother who came first, got a job, sent money home, and then the next one would come, and the next one.

When my grandfather finally arrived, each of his brothers chipped in a little money and bought him a paint store in Williamsburg. The sign on the store said SOLOMON'S PAINTS. My grandfather found out it would cost five dollars to change the name on the sign from Solomon to Dworetsky, and he said forget it.

That's how his name got to be Solomon. From a sign outside a store that his brothers bought for him. In time, the brothers changed their name from Dworetsky to Dworkin and from Dworkin to Dorsey, but Solomon remained my grandfather's name.

Even before my family moved in with him, my mother insisted we visit his house every Sunday, out of respect. We kids would be sent to play in another room, away from the grown-ups, and we'd fight and carry on, but the minute we grew silent, my grandfather, certain that we were up to no good, would come knocking on our closed door. "Vot's vid de qviet in dere?"

All of us used to gather around and watch the radio. Isn't that weird? You could hear it if your back was turned, couldn't you? Yet everybody would take chairs and sit and watch the radio. And there were so many children, so many relatives, it was so crowded I slept with two other kids in a bed. Still, I remember it as fun. I mean a five-, six-, seven-year-old kid doesn't know he's underprivileged.

But for my father, it wasn't fun. To the end, he nourished his loathing for my mother's family. When he was eighty, he had to go for prostate surgery, and everybody was worried, it was very scary. Eventually, he was wheeled out of the operating room, and the surgeon said he'd come through very well, but my mother wanted to make sure. "I need to go in and see him." So they let her into the recovery room and she came out a few minutes later, crying.

"My God," I said, "what happened?"

"He's cursing my brother Nat," she said.

"What?"

"He's cursing my brother Nat. What does he want from my brother Nat? Nat's been dead for forty years."

So I went in and asked him, "What do you want from Mom? Why are you cursing her brother Nat? Nat's been dead for forty years." And my father said, "Dead don't make you better."

That's the way he was. He saw so much bullshit, and he was an iconoclast. Whatever you were for, he was against. My mother's father was a rabbi? My father became an atheist. But growing up, I had the best of both of them.

I really think of myself as two people, Alan King and Irwin Kniberg. My life has been like a Dalí painting, very strange, fragmented; it's got three eyes and four arms and a lot of breasts. My mother was a big-breasted woman, and all my life I've been attracted to—but that's another story. This kid, Irwin Kniberg, is still inside there, desperate, wanting to do something, be somebody. That need made me impossible.

My first experience on a stage with an audience came in public school. We did Tom Sawyer, and I played Huck Finn. Aunt Polly was a girl by the name of Ruth Zatz. But by now I was already singing and dancing on street corners, doing impersonations for pennies. Somebody would take a penny and fold tissue paper around it (oranges used to come wrapped in that paper), and throw it out the window.

So I was always in the street. I used to get all the kids sitting on milk boxes—ten, twelve kids—and I'd tell them stories I made up. My father was a great storyteller, and I inherited that ability. On Saturdays, I spent from morning to night in the movie theater. The New Broadway. Kids could get in two for a nickel. I'd steal a milk bottle, get two cents' deposit back, then stand under the marquee bawling, "I got two, who's got three?"

I knew I was different. I was always in trouble, always fighting, I hated school, I was always up before the principal. I'd come in late, make an excuse, somebody in the class would laugh, and I'd nail him. I was a very angry, very tough kid, I don't know why. In the streets, I was a little gang leader, because I could make people listen. "That's what being important is," my father said. "When people will listen to you."

He was totally supportive of me, his gangster. If I kicked a football in the schoolyard, this Russian-Polish immigrant would come down to watch me do it, though he didn't know the first thing about the game. "Be a somebody," he'd tell me again and again. "You gotta be a somebody. The greatest gift I've given you is that I'm nothing, so you got no footsteps to follow in."

Because he'd had all these dreams that never came true.

He was forever advising me to escape. "Get the hell out of this house, get the hell out of this neighborhood, even if it means leaving school. Stay here, and you'll end up like me, all you'll have to show for forty years of working is a machine by the window."

On the other hand, he was no stage father, he just wanted me to do what I wanted to do. And what I wanted to do was be an actor. Sometimes my mother would walk in on me emoting in front of a mirror, and she'd scream, "Bernie, look what we got here, anodder Paul Muni."

But the rest of her family, the rest of the community, for that matter, didn't think of me as an actor, they said my father spoiled me rotten and I was going to be a bum. (When I went to Washington to emcee the gala for Jack Kennedy's inauguration, my parents were already living in Florida, and my father wished he could be back in the old neighborhood, lording it over the old neighbors. "Hah? See? There he is—the *bum*—with the president of the United States!")

My mother didn't think I was a bum, but she and everybody else used to say, "You're just like your father." They meant that as something terrible; I took it as a compliment. It was my father and me against the world. Especially when his in-laws butted in. That's all he needed, somebody to tell him what to do with *his* son. My mother deeply disapproved of my acting ambitions, but he wouldn't listen. "Let him be," he'd tell her. "He'll outgrow it." Until the day she died, my mother was waiting for me to outgrow it and get a real job.

Most comedians are angry, it's their edge, and when I was small, I took out some of my rage in drumming. At the time I started playing drums, my father had a job on the Lower East Side, and there was a trolley that took people across the Williamsburg Bridge to the city. It cost three cents to ride, so my father walked across the bridge every morning. He always walked one way, and the three cents a day that he saved went to pay the New York School for Music for my drum lessons. We couldn't afford drums at home, so I practiced by beating up the chairs.

By the time I was ten, I had my own band. I called it Earl Knight and the Musical Knights. At school, there was this wonderful teacher, Dorothy Berkfeld, and when she knew I had a gig on Saturday night, she would tell me, "You close up the music room," turn her back, and I would steal the bass drum and the snare drum, take them to the job, and return them Monday morning.

Even before that, I had met the woman I would marry. Jeanette's family were the elite of the neighborhood, the only people who had a car. Her father was in the monument business—Sprung Monuments, they made gravestones—and neither he nor Mrs. Sprung approved when I started coming around to see Jeanette. I was eleven, she was ten, and her parents, who knew my reputation as the worst kid in the neighborhood, used to lock her in her room.

I don't blame them. If my daughter had brought home a kid like me, I'd have locked her in too. I usually showed up with a bloody nose from fighting some other small tough.

Often the fight was in defense of my friend Alex Jabofsky. He couldn't beat an old wino with a bad cough but he was always getting into fights and I'd have to save him. He was my best friend. His father, a plumber, always seemed to be hanging around their house in his long underwear with the trap door open and his backside hanging out.

Mr. Jabofsky knew I was interested in show business, and one day when I came over, he told me about having been to the Yiddish theater. "I went to see your friend, Menasha Skulnik, yesterday. I gave him good."

A famous comedian, Menasha Skulnik used to come onstage and say to the audience, *"Du kenst mir?"* ("You know me?") and everybody would applaud. So I said to Mr. Jabofsky, "Whaddaya mean, you gave him good?" And Mr. Jabofsky said, "Menasha came out and he looked at us and he said, 'You know me?' and I shouted back, 'Go take a good shit for yourself!' "

Some masterful ad-lib. Poor Alex was so embarrassed he wanted to fall out of the window.

Still determined to make somebody besides my father admire me (band jobs were few and far between), I started doing little things around town, entering amateur contests, being a singing usher, and all my mother's friends would say, "I knew it, I knew it, you know how he used to stand there and tell all them stories?"

Even my grandfather, the rabbi, visited one of the local movie houses where I was appearing in a variety show, but he didn't want anyone to see him in such a sinful place. He and two of my uncles walked in after the lights were down, and stood at the back of the house.

But by the time my grandfather returned to his congregation, the word had got out, and somebody said, "I know you went to see your grandson, so tell me, what does he do?" And in Yiddish, my grandfather said, "Well, I don't know, he stands on the stage and makes funny noises and shakes his ass."

All these years later, when somebody asks me what I do, I say, "I stand on the stage, make funny noises, and shake my ass."

I think my father might have liked my grandfather if he'd given himself half a chance. But the difference between my grandfather and my father is, my father was so bitter. That was the saddest part. He was kind to everybody, everyone adored him for his wit, but he carried with him such anger against my mother's family, because he hadn't made good. Sometimes I tried to reason with him. "You'd better stop blaming everybody else, and settle down and enjoy what you have. Don't keep saying your brother-in-law didn't let you do this or that."

In time, he came to live vicariously, through me. When I was on the road, he'd go down to the corner gas station where they gave away maps. He'd collect the maps, take them home, and study them. He knew where Utica was, how many miles it was to Harrisburg. He'd tell me, "You're going to have to take Ninety-one."

As I got older, it remained the same. When I was at the height of my career, very successful, making a lot of money, every time my father saw me, he asked, "How's prospects?" And he gave me advice. He never made eighty dollars a week in his life, and he was telling me what to do with my money. "You watching it? You taking care of it?"

In a way, he was a tragic figure, but he had a great sense of humor, and he never kidded himself. And he was so smart, I've known Nobel Prize winners and Pulitzer Prize winners who weren't as smart, but as he grew old, he became disillusioned about politics, socialism, everything he had once believed in, and there was a lot of mea culpa.

Always, though, he said interesting things. "I never met anybody I liked who wasn't a little crazy," he said. "Never trust a clergyman that has more than one suit," he said.

My father could cut to the bone.

I loved him, but I couldn't wait to hit the road. During my adolescence, *Major Bowes' Amateur Hour* was the biggest show on radio. Sinatra had been a Major Bowes winner, and Vic Damone and Robert Merrill and Marilyn Horne; it was quite a springboard. I auditioned, was chosen to be a contestant, came onstage with a dirty face, in torn knickers, cap askew, newspapers under my arm, and sang "Brother, Can You Spare a Dime?" Grown men wept.

I lost to a musical plumber from Poughkeepsie, but the Major used to take out tours—he'd mix up winners and losers and transport them all over the country—and he offered me a job with one of his traveling shows. He said since I was underage, we'd take along a tutor—the tutor turned out to be a drunk, but that didn't bother me—and I'd be paid thirty-five dollars a week. It was more than my father was making.

A day doesn't go by that I don't think of my youth, and yet I was never a kid. I was fourteen when I promised my mother I'd go back to school as soon as my tour with the Major was over, but she knew I was leaving home. I mean, I was out of there. On my way to try to be somebody.

2 ∽ The World of Summer

The mountain nymph, sweet Liberty.

—JOHN MILTON

AFTER I CAME HOME from my tour with Major Bowes, my mother called in her marker. I'd sworn I would finish my education, and she wanted to see some evidence that my word could be trusted.

So I tried to go back to school. And I got thrown out. I got thrown out of Boys' High, I got thrown out of Eastern District High, I got thrown out of every high school my mother came up with. I just couldn't sit there anymore. I mean, I'd gotten *laid* in Chicago. I'd been living in hotels, eating in restaurants, performing for audiences. Now, seven, eight months later, what school could I fit into? Where was I going to matriculate?

The Catskill Mountains, affectionately called the borscht circuit, became my high school. But being on the road with the Major had broadened my horizons. I didn't want to work in the mountains with a band, I wanted to be a comedian. So I went back to hanging around the streets. I knew a lot of guys, I'd hear who was auditioning. There was a man by the name of Mike Hammer—he was a legendary mountain booker, he had found the tenor Jan Peerce, when Jan Peerce was Pinky Perlman—and he was hiring for the Hotel Gradus. I sang some comedy songs for him, and he asked me if I'd like to be on the Gradus staff.

I went up for Memorial Day, got onstage, and did a joke.

"When you work for Gradus," I said, "you work for gratis." Everybody laughed except Mr. Gradus, the owner of the hotel. He didn't know what I was talking about. Then somebody explained it to him, and he fired me. In the middle of the night, I had to leave.

I walked to a place called the Kentucky Club, quite some distance away, in Woodbridge. Somebody told me a lot of actors and agents gathered there, and I might be able to get a lift home; there were always cars going back.

So I was looking for a ride, and I met these two funny little men, Max Metzger and Morris Bleiman, two refugees from Europe, with heavy accents, and one of them said, "Vot do you do?"

"I just got fired," I said.

"Go up dere and do a turn," he said, and he asked Henry Berman, the club's featured performer, to introduce me to the audience. (Berman was known as the Jewish Harry Richman; the fact that Harry Richman was also Jewish seemed never to have occurred to anybody.)

I launched into a routine I'd stolen from Willie Howard, the great, great stage comedian, who was one of my father's favorites. It was a man on a soapbox making a speech, and it started, "Fellow voikers, comes the revolution—"

I got laughs, and Max and Morris said, "Don't go home, we'll get you a room here, you'll stay till tomorrow."

The next day, they took me over to the New Prospect Hotel and introduced me to the owner, Mrs. Gatkin. "We got a boy here—"

She hired me. I was the number three comic, the porch tummler, I ran around and did crazy things. I entertained all day long, in the dining room, on the lawn, and they'd give me a little part in the show. I used to emcee the beauty contest; my big joke was about how ugly the contestants were. "For the first time in the history of beauty contests, there will be no winners."

They paid me ten dollars a week, a hundred dollars for the season, and when it was over, Mrs. Gatkin said, "I'd like you to come back next year. You'll be the number one comic. You'll still be under the social director, but you'll be the number one comic."

For several summers, I worked all over the Catskills, and in the winters, I worked in Lakewood, New Jersey. The classiest hotel in Lakewood, Laurel in the Pines, was owned by the mother of Larry and Bob Tisch, who eventually headed CBS and Loew's.

Mrs. Tisch was tough. I remember one afternoon when a lot of old folks were sitting around on the porch, wrapped up in blankets as if they were on an ocean voyage, and I was trying to get everybody's blood moving, tummling, doing my shtick, when Mrs. Tisch happened along. "Young man," she said, "save your antics for the stage. This is Laurel in the Pines, not the Borscht Belt."

It took a while, but Mrs. Tisch finally paid me a compliment. "You're pretty funny," she told me, adding, "Stay out of the girls' dressing room!"

People ask if those were the days when I started writing my own material. I wasn't writing material, I wasn't writing anything. At the time, I couldn't even spell. I still can't spell, and I didn't read my first book until I was seventeen years old. It was *A Stone for Danny Fisher,* about growing up in Brooklyn in a tough neighborhood, and I thought it was my life story.

Then I read *Zorba the Greek,* where Zorba says to this writer he works for something like, "You know, boss, you got everything except you have no insanity, and without a little insanity, you can never pull the rope." It was what my father always said, you need to be a little crazy to get the best out of everything, and that was Zorba's philosophy too. Would you believe it? I asked myself. This guy, Nikos Kazantzakis, is stealing from my old man.

Having discovered that reading was the most entertaining thing I could do, I went through two, three books at a time. I couldn't get enough; I began reading everything with a dictionary beside me, like I was a foreigner. I discovered Saul Bellow and Clifford Odets. Up till then, I thought everybody wrote like Faulkner or Shakespeare. I didn't know there were people around writing about delinquents like me.

But all this didn't start till later. As I said, I was fifteen when I first went to the mountains as a comedian, and it was great. Anything I wanted to do I could do. No mother, no father bothering me, and the world of summer.

In those Catskill resorts, you put on a vaudeville show one night, a burlesque show the next night, you did a musical, an operetta, and a show where you got all the guests to perform, and let them make schmucks of themselves.

I went through forty phases in my life. There were forty Alan Kings. I started out as a kind of burlesque comedian—burlesque was very physical—and later when I saw Milton Berle, he became my idol. Brash, with the cigar, even before he became Mr. Television, he was the biggest variety star in the world.

Great comics—Jackie Miles, Jan Murray, Phil Foster—worked the Catskills, and I soaked them up. I stole from everyone. I did Milton Berle's act, and Jerry Lester's. I did all the guys, I did Danny Kaye. Danny Kaye was in Hollywood, and I was working at a shithouse in Fallsburg, New York, how was I going to hurt Danny Kaye? Jerry Lester was working the Paramount, and I was working a bust-out joint in New Jersey, who was I hurting?

I'd change styles after I'd see somebody new, and yet, essentially, I was still doing Milton.

But I'd try anything. I came down out of the mountains and worked on the famous Steel Pier, for the diving horse, the greatest attraction that ever played Atlantic City. I think of myself, that fifteen-year-old barker in white flannels with a bamboo cane and a straw sailor hat, announcing, "The eighth wonder of the world, high atop the cruel Atlantic!" The people would pay a quarter apiece, and they'd line up for hours to see the horse jump into a tank of water way down below; we did six shows a day.

The handlers would take the horse, put a cinch around it, and crank it up to a diving ledge sixty feet in the air. They'd do a drumroll, and the owner would take an electric prod and shove it up the horse's ass, and the horse would dive. I still can't believe anybody thought a horse would jump of his own volition sixty feet into the water, but the crowds kept coming.

When I wasn't working, the movies were still my great escape, my Hans Christian Andersen, my Arabian Nights. And the only person I knew who could remember as much movie dialogue as I could was Sammy Davis Jr. We acted out whole pages, whole scenes; we drove everybody crazy.

I met Sammy around Broadway, when he and I were hanging out in the different cafeterias where all the actors went. Though we were close in age, he was already a headliner (as part of the Will Mastin Trio) with his uncle and his father. I loved Sammy—lots of people loved Sammy—but he found it hard to trust that affection; he came with a lot of baggage. Onstage, he was a star; offstage, he had to use a side door to get into his hotel.

It was different for me. Growing up, I didn't know from bigotry. Literally. I went from living in a ghetto where everybody was Jewish to a school where everybody was Jewish. I thought the whole world was Jewish until I was fourteen, when I went on the road, and realized it wasn't.

On the road, I learned about prejudice. It wasn't only people of color who were discriminated against; I heard people refer to me as "that Jew comic," and for a while, in my act, I tried to be more white-bread, more Waspy. It didn't work, it wasn't me. I finally said, Screw it, and after that, I wore my Jewishness like a badge of honor.

And I needed armor, because my determination to have a theatrical career continued to be an aggravation to my mother. (I guess we're using the term *career* loosely when we're talking about playing straight man to a diving horse.) My mother was always running to my grandfather, the rabbi, to back her up in her arguments with me. Often he settled things in a very Talmudic way. (The Talmud has two answers for every question.) Here's an example:

In the days before World War II, the idea of flying seemed insane to people who lived in a poor ghetto neighborhood; it was considered daredevil stuff. Well, I had the mountains in the summer, and eventually I would go, like all the other comedians, to play clubs in Florida in the winter, but at this time, I was still hustling any little jobs I could get. And I had a phone call from an agent who said a comedian had got sick in Albany, and if I wanted to sub for him, I would have to fly up to Albany that day.

I told my mother, who went into hysterics. She always reacted to everything by threatening, "I'll kill myself!" As if killing herself would make everything all right. So she says, "You can't fly, come, we'll talk to Grandpa."

I go in to see Grandpa, and he launches into a sermon. "Why do you need to go on an airplane? The world is going to hell because everybody's rushing.

"Do you know they have a lovely train that goes from New York to Albany? You get on the train, you take a nice book, you'll have the opportunity to read.

"The train has a dining car. You'll sit down, have a sandwich.

"Do you know that the train to Albany stops in Poughkeepsie? And do you know that you have an aunt that lives in Poughkeepsie? You'll call your aunt and tell her you're coming—the train probably stops in Poughkeepsie for twenty minutes—and she'll meet you at the station, and you'll have a visit with an aunt you haven't seen in twelve years. You will then arrive in Albany relaxed, fresh, ready to do what you have to do."

I've been listening respectfully, and now I say, "But Grandpa, in order for me to get the job, I gotta be there tonight."

"Well then," he says, "you'll take an airplane."

After Albany, I went north, to Montreal. I had a buddy who was working there, a singer named Alan Dale, and he told me he could get me a job at the Gaiety Burlesque house, a famous theater on St. Catherine Street.

The year was 1943, by then the war was on, and you could visit Canada, though if you wanted to stay, you had to report to the local police station and state your business. I neglected to take care of this matter, but Alan Dale got me an audition, and there I was with a job in the burlesque show. You know what that was like? I'm sixteen years old, there are naked women running around, it was forget about it, wow!

One of the strippers, she was called Princess Wah Wah—she was supposed to be an Indian—took a liking to me, and I had a romance with her. It was like a dream, like I'd gone to heaven. Then one day, there were two guys in uniforms, immigration officers, standing backstage. "Where's your papers?" one of them said.

I didn't have any papers, I wasn't even using my real name. I was calling myself Alan Knight. The officers said I had to leave the country, they were going to put me on a train. I wasn't under arrest or anything, it wasn't a handcuff situation, but I wasn't ready to go home. It was my fourth week in the burlesque house, I had a little money, so I just took off, running, and escaped.

There was a place called the Windsor Steak House in downtown Montreal where we used to go after the show, take the girls for a drink. It was in an old brownstone; downstairs there was a big bar, and upstairs a restaurant.

Harry Labe, the guy who owned it, had been a middleweight fighter at one time, and he used to have a lot of fighters around. When he found out I was on the lam, he offered to help. He knew I was pretty good with my hands—in the daytime, he'd seen me working out in the gym—and he thought he could get me some fights. "You'll come up to Quebec City with me," he said, "we'll get you fifty dollars, you'll fight a few three-rounders."

(On the Lower East Side, I'd boxed at the Education Alliance. That neighborhood house was a great place; it got kids off the streets, and there were instructors to teach you basketball, handball, boxing. I wasn't Sugar Ray Robinson, but there was a lot of violence in me, I was pugnacious.)

So Harry Labe and I went off to Quebec City, and he got me a fight, and I won the fight. After that, we traveled around Canada for about six months. I fought once or twice a week. These were club fights, professional, you got paid for it. (Amateur fights you didn't get paid; they used to give you a watch and there was a guy outside who'd buy the watch from you for twenty dollars.) I was making fifty dollars, a hundred dollars, a fight, and I'd box under a different name every time.

I'd had about twenty fights, and won every one of them. I had been moving up a little bit in class, and then I got to Hamilton, Ontario, where I was to box in a movie house. (It was a regular proscenium theater, the audience wasn't all around you.) My opponent was a black kid, two heads taller than I was, thin as a rail, and he had hands that went from one end of the ring to the other.

His name was King, and he beat me to within an inch of my life, he just tore me apart. And I said to Harry Labe, "There's gotta be a better way for a nice Jewish boy to make a living."

(In fact, a lot of the fighters who were my heroes—Barney Ross, Benny Leonard, Ruby Goldstein—were Jewish. And everybody told me Max Baer was Jewish because he wore a Jewish star, but that was just a good luck thing. He'd borrowed trunks with a Star of David on them and won the fight, and after that he always wore them. His brother Buddy was a Roman Catholic, so how could Max be Jewish?)

So now I said, "Harry, I gotta get out of here, this is not for me," and I went back to New York, and this skinny big-handed fighter, King, went on to become the lightweight champion of Canada.

There's a postscript to this story. Many, many, many years later, I'm on *The Tonight Show*—I'd actually taken the name King from the guy that beat me—and Johnny Carson says to me, "I hear you had a limited boxing career." I say yeah, and I tell him some funny stories about my fights, and about King battering me, and how I woke up in the dressing room and realized my boxing career was over. "You know," I say to Johnny, "when I think about it, I owe this guy King a great deal of thanks for beating me up."

About three months afterward, I get a letter. It's been to NBC, and then to the Carson show, and then to the William Morris agency. It's written like Charlie Brown, with the inverted letters, all in crayon. It was from King. He had a shoeshine stand in the Brown Building in Toronto, and he said since I owed him so much, how about sending him five thousand dollars?

By coincidence, Brownie, the guy who owned the Brown Building, was a friend of mine, and I picked up the phone and called him in Toronto. I told him the whole story—he hadn't seen the Carson show—and he said, "Yeah, we got a punch-drunk fighter who shines shoes in the lobby. And yeah, he was a champion. King, that's right."

I mailed Brownie a check for five hundred dollars and told him to give it to King. Brownie called me after he received the money. "That guy's not so punchy," he said. "He called you a cheap bastard."

But he cashed the check.

3 ∞ THE ENTERTAINER

"I'm a comedian."
"I'll be the judge of that."

WHEN I LEFT CANADA, most of the American comedians were in the army, so suddenly there was a lot of work for an underage hopeful. I set my sights on Leon and Eddie's, a 52nd Street club that was owned and run by an entertainer named Eddie Davis and his partner, Leon Enken. Davis used to sing risqué songs, he was kind of like a Joe E. Lewis. Right next door to Leon and Eddie's was the "21" Club, and across the street was Jack White's 18 Club, which had been a speakeasy. Before it became Swing Street, 52nd Street was all speakeasies.

All during World War II, Leon and Eddie's put on four shows a night. Sunday was Celebrity Night. They'd honor a well-known entertainer, and all the friends of the entertainer would get up and do turns, and every agent, every manager in town would be there.

Celebrity Night started around 11 P.M. and went till six o'clock in the morning. Every once in a while, Eddie Davis would let a wannabe take the stage. It was a great showcase; I used to read about it in Walter Winchell's column, Lee Mortimer's column, Danton Walker's column, Ed Sullivan's column.

I didn't have any money to come into the city and go drinking—I was still flopping (in more ways than one) at my parents' Brooklyn apartment—but I could always lay my hands on a quarter. So one Sunday night I took the subway to Manhattan (a nickel), spent two cents on the *Daily News* and two cents on the *Daily Mirror*, and went to Horn & Hardart, the automat where for a dime you could get a roll and the best baked beans that were ever made. Then I headed for Leon and Eddie's.

My mother was still making noises about my going back to school, but that was out of the question. I knew that everything that interested me was at Leon and Eddie's, and I just wanted to smell it.

There was a big rectangular bar at the back of the room; it was packed on this Sunday night, and I mingled with the people who were standing in front of it two, three deep, and watched the show. Whenever I thought the bartender was becoming suspicious, I'd move to another part of the bar. I got away with it that first time, and I got away with it a second time, and both times, I went home and told my pals everybody I'd seen—Bill "Bojangles" Robinson, Martha Raye, John Barrymore—everybody.

Barrymore almost broke my heart, because in his old age, he was a drunk, pure and simple. He'd been a famous romantic actor who became a sort of cartoon character, playing parts in which he made fun of himself and his boozing. I'd never seen him in person (though I knew him from the *Sealtest Radio Hour*) until he staggered through the door of Leon and Eddie's at about one in the morning.

He was being held up by Victor Jory and John Carradine, and all three actors were loaded. The maître d', Louis Katz, and Eddie Davis ran over and seated them, but Barrymore fell right off his chair.

It was the most embarrassing scene, and all of a sudden I heard Eddie Davis say, "Ladies and gentlemen, the greatest actor in the world, John Barrymore," and Barrymore tried to get up and take a bow, but he couldn't do it. The spotlight was searching the room, Jory and Carradine were trying to help him, and they were falling all over each other.

There was an ovation from the show business audience, and Barrymore finally managed to find his way to the stage. When he hit the light, everyone realized he was bombed, and the room went silent. He stumbled to the mike and, pulling himself together, began to speak with Shakespearean diction, rolling his *r*'s, broadening his *a*'s.

"It has been," he said, "many years since I was in Leon and Eddie's. The last time I was here, I was drinking." He got a laugh, and continued.

"And as I walked down Fifty-second Street, the street became a path in the Garden of Eden. And the canopies on all the nightclubs along the street became tents out of the *Arabian Nights*. And as I walked through the door, Louis Katz became a maharaja, and when I was invited up on the stage, I looked out at the audience, and the men were all Romeo and the women were all Juliet. But then, as I say, I was drinking.

"Standing here before you tonight, completely sober, may I tell you, you are the ugliest bastards I have ever seen in my life."

And he walked off, making an exit like only a Barrymore could.

I remember another fabled Broadway star, James Barton, taking that same stage to sing "Waitin' for the *Robert E. Lee*." He could sing as well as Al Jolson, and that was the night that Bill Robinson, who was in the audience, got up and danced while Barton sang.

James Barton is little remembered today, but he was an incredible artist. He wore a putty nose—his own nose had been eaten away by syphilis—and he used to do a comedy number about a drunk who runs out of money and is thrown out of a bar. He's lying on the sidewalk when a dog comes by and sniffs him, and he gets an idea. He walks back into the bar with a handkerchief wrapped around his hand, says, "I was just bitten by a mad dog," and the bartender gives him a drink.

So he goes into every bar on the street, and tells the same story. And you see him up there onstage getting drunker and drunker, until he's mumbling about elephants and alligators, and bouncing around on his rubber legs, and finally, not realizing he's making a mistake, he goes back into the first bar. Again he's thrown out. Again he's lying on the sidewalk, again the dog walks by, and Barton says to the dog, "Don't go in there, they're wise to us."

Well, for a couple of weeks, I lived in a fool's paradise, watching those shows and never having to buy so much as a beer, but when I came back the third week, somebody tapped me on the shoulder. I turned and saw this tall man; it was Eddie Davis. "What are you doing here?" he said.

I was dressed nicely, so I bluffed. "What do you mean, what am I doing here?"

He told me what he meant. "You haven't bought a drink in three weeks." (Louis Katz, the maître d', had turned me in; he had eyes in the back of his head.)

I said, "Mr. Davis, I'm a comedian/entertainer," and he said, "I'll be the judge of that."

He took me upstairs to his office, where he had a little rehearsal piano, and he had Art Wayner, who was his piano player and bandleader, come with us. Eddie asked me what I wanted to do, and I suggested a number called "Babalu." Miguelito Valdez, who sang with Xavier Cugat, had a big hit record with "Babalu," and I used to do a satire on that, a takeoff on a Cuban singer.

Art Wayner sat down at the piano, Eddie Davis sat down at his desk, and I did the song. Then Art went back to the bandstand, I went back to the bar, and Celebrity Night began. After a while, I heard Eddie Davis tell the audience, "We have a young entertainer here tonight," and he called me up to the stage. I was too dumb to be frightened, I had the balls of a lion, and I sang "Babalu" and broke up the joint.

Afterward, Davis asked me where I worked. I told him I was looking for a job. He said, "Come back and see me on Tuesday night." Then he walked me to the door. "How much money have you got in your pocket?"

"A lot," I said. He nodded. "Show me how much money you got."

I had six cents, more than enough to get to Brooklyn, but Eddie Davis walked me to a cab—there was a line of cabs outside the club waiting for all the big-time people—and he went up to the first driver in line and said, "Take this kid home."

I was shocked. "Mr. Davis, I live in Brooklyn—"

"I don't care," he said, handing the driver some folding money. So six o'clock in the morning, my mother, who always worried about me, was looking out the window, and I pulled up in a cab. Nobody in my family had ever ridden in a taxi before.

I told my parents the story; my father was thrilled, my mother didn't believe it.

Tuesday night, I went back to see Eddie Davis, and he bought me dinner. He was a kind man. The long and short of it is, he gave me a job as assistant doorman. Then on Sunday nights, he'd tell the audience, "We have a very funny doorman," and I would come onstage in my uniform and sing and do impressions.

Leon and Eddie's was always jammed. Sherry Britton, a famous stripper, worked there, along with a line of beautiful chorus girls, so the place was packed with servicemen. Eddie Davis would call a bunch of them up on the stage and lead them through a number called "Hands, Feet, and Bumps-a-Daisy," the servicemen banging backsides with the chorus girls. That was a surefire crowd pleaser. Another winner was an act Joey Adams used to do with Mark Plant, Tony Canzoneri (the ex-fighter), and Horace McMahon, a tough guy in the movies. The four of them would impersonate the Ink Spots.

Soon I was performing weeknights as well as Sundays. Eddie Davis did the eight o'clock show and the midnight show, and he let me work the ten o'clock show and the 2:30 A.M. show. He always fed me and sent me home in a cab with twenty dollars. And I got to know everybody in the business.

In my parents' apartment on Bedford Avenue in Brooklyn, there was only one bedroom, and with my new-earned wealth, I bought my mother a bedroom set at Ludwig Baumann's. It was a famous store, you could pay off your bill at two dollars, three dollars a week. I would come home from Leon and Eddie's at dawn, my mother and father would get up, and I'd fall into the bed. (My sister was already married and out of the house.)

During the days, I did a lot of weight lifting and boxing. When I was sixteen I was as big as I am now (I had already boxed a 165-pounder), and I would go to the St. George Hotel, which had an indoor swimming pool. It cost ten cents to go swimming, and I liked to show off for the girls there. I used to walk around the pool doing all that muscle-flexing kind of bullshit too.

I took Jeanette to the St. George pool on our first real date. Up till then we'd been sneaking around; we'd meet each other in the movies, or on a street corner, and my friends all used to make fun of me. They thought she was stuck-up because she never smiled, and since her father was in the monument business, they called her "Stone Face." But my father liked her. Being the richest girl in the neighborhood, she was a somebody.

Anyway, Jeanette's brother Hy found out I had taken his sister to the St. George against their parents' wishes, and I hadn't got her home until after dark. She and I were sitting on a stoop around the corner from her house, when all of a sudden, three guys came to the bottom of the steps. Her brother had sent them to teach me a lesson.

"Go home," one of them told Jeanette, who got frightened and started to cry.

I stood up. "You guys are out of line."

"Never mind out of line," one bellowed, "you come down here."

I put on a show of bravado. "If you'll come over here one at a time, I'll beat the shit out of all three of you."

I'm daring them, and Jeanette's standing there; she doesn't want to abandon me. Across the street on the corner there's a movie theater, the RKO Republic, and as I'm talking to these three young punks, the movie breaks, and in the light spill from the lobby, I see Alex Jabofsky and a kid called Herbie Moon. I scream, "Bof!" and Alex and Herbie come running over, and despite the fact that Alex's enthusiasm is a lot stronger than his fists, we take these three guys apart, leave them for dead.

Now these three guys were looking for me every day. I used to shoot craps for pennies, and I was trapped in an alley the night they caught up with me. Nobody in that crap game was going to help me, and the three guys kept coming. One of the crap shooters had a baseball bat, and I grabbed it, and took on those three guys again. And beat them. It was terrible. Not compared to what kids do today—we didn't have guns and knives—but pretty bad, and my reputation became even worse. To Jeanette's mother and father, I was the local killer.

Right after that, I stopped using my fists and started using my wits, a more powerful weapon. Comedy gives you tremendous power.

I was still working at Leon and Eddie's when I met Georgie Jay. He had a club called Georgie Jay's 78th Street Tap Room, and he offered me seventy-five dollars a week to do three shows a night there. "It's a rough joint, but I think you can handle it."

It *was* a rough joint, a hangout for pimps, hoodlums, and ex-fighters. (Every time I saw a broken nose, a cauliflower ear, or heard a stutter in some guy's speech pattern, I knew I'd made the right choice when I gave up fighting.) But I was seventeen, and I was excited. This was a real job. Georgie would advertise in the papers on Friday and Saturday nights; my name was going to be in print for the first time.

For my opening I needed a new suit, so my parents and my uncle Louis took me down to the Lower East Side. Every immigrant family had a smart-guy uncle, the expert, the one who used to kick the tires, like the car was going to fall down. Uncle Louis was the suit maven. He'd take every suit out into the street and look at it in the daylight. I'd say, "Uncle Louis, why are you taking it outside? I'm gonna wear it in a dark nightclub."

Suitably attired in blue serge—it would have been fine for a bar mitzvah—I opened at Georgie Jay's. In between shows, the entertainment was provided by Johnny Dee, who was a singing waiter. He played the piano—it was on wheels, a busboy pushed it around—and he'd sing to the customers and they'd put money in the kitty.

One night, when I was on my break, Johnny Dee invited me to sing along with him. "You can pick up some extra money." He was right. There was one patron who loved "Let the Rest of the World Go By" and he'd drop in maybe once a month, drunk, then slip me a twenty to sing it.

Many of the great fighters of the time used to come by. I met Rocky Graziano, Willie Pep, Tony Janero, Lou Ambers, and I became a favorite at that little place. My big number was "Ace in the Hole." I could tear the hell out of that. I'd be wailing, "This town is fulla guys that think they're mighty wise," and all these hoodlums would be crying. One night I hit the last note, and some drunk stood up and said, "Didn't I see you box in Canada?"

I said yes.

"You were a better fighter than you are a singer," he said. He considered this for a few seconds. "And," he added sorrowfully, "you stunk as a fighter."

I had been at the 78th Street Tap Room a couple of weeks, when I invited my mother and father and my uncle Hymie and Jeanette to come see me. Jeanette was still in high school; she had to finish her homework before she could leave the house.

I'd stolen a number from Jerry Lester, who had stolen it from Harry Lauder, the Scottish comedian. Jerry rolled his pants up to his knees, took off his suit jacket, wrapped it around his waist, and tied the sleeves in the back so it looked like he was wearing a kilt.

The night my family came, I was doing the Jerry Lester bit, getting big laughs, and in the middle of the act, above the laughter, I could hear my mother's voice. She was wailing, "Oh my God, look what he's doing to his new suit."

I was a Broadway kid now, and I had a manager named Lou Perry. He didn't want me to keep commuting to Brooklyn. "That's a terrible schlepp every night."

It was true. I remember coming off the subway, the elevated train, in Williamsburg about six o'clock one morning, and Jeanette's father was on his way to his shop, and he saw me. One more black mark against the loser who wanted to steal away his daughter.

"Come on," Lou Perry said. "You'll move in with us."

"Us" was Dean Martin (an ex-fighter) and a guy named Sonny King (who went to work with Jimmy Durante after Eddie Jackson left the act). Sonny was a popular singer and, strangely enough, another ex-fighter. The three of us got better write-ups in *Ring* magazine than we did in *Variety*.

We were all being managed by Lou and sharing—along with Lou—one room in the Bryant Hotel. It was on 54th Street and Broadway. (Later it became a welfare hotel, but it's been remodeled and has some foreign name now.) It was two blocks from Lindy's and right down the street from the Royal Roost, a jazz joint.

Our room had one bed and a foldout couch. We slept two on the bed and two on the couch. If a fifth person stayed over (Lou also handled a comedian named Henny Nadel who did a routine with a pickle, and he was there sometimes), the guy who came in last slept in the bathtub.

To us, 52nd Street seemed like the hub of the world. Every club had an awning, every club had a doorman who sounded like a carnival barker. Billie Holiday, Art Tatum, Sidney Bechet, Erroll Garner, all the great jazz stars played 52nd Street. Toots Shor, who had been a bouncer at Leon and Eddie's, opened his own place right next door.

I'd moved up from Kellogg's Cafeteria to Lindy's, where Milton Berle occupied the front table with his hangers-on. Walter Winchell used to share a booth with Damon Runyon, who had lost his voice to cancer; now he sat silent, writing funny notes.

Ed Weiner, my first press agent, convinced Winchell to put me in the column. (Once a week he ran a paragraph headed "Orchids to . . ." and getting mentioned in that paragraph was like getting an Academy Award.)

"Orchids to Alan King, 78th Street Tap Room." That was—forget about it. Now nobody, not the neighbors, not my uncles, could tell my mother I was born to be a gangster. I had been ordained by Walter Winchell.

Winchell spent his winters in Miami, at the magnificent Roney Plaza Hotel on 23rd Street and Collins Avenue—Miami Beach was the Las Vegas of the forties and fifties—and every afternoon he held court in the Bamboo Room of the Roney, surrounded by America's power brokers, including the FBI chief, J. Edgar Hoover.

When I was booked into the Famous Door, a rat-trap strip joint down the street, I made it a point to get by the Bamboo Room every day, stop at Winchell's table, and tell a couple of jokes. (My first job in Miami had been at the Olympia Theater. I played there in a major hurricane and wrote a joke about it. A guy's standing in front of a hotel during the storm, and he says, "I wonder who's playing at the Olympia," and the hotel doorman says, "Wait a minute, here comes the marquee now.")

One of the regulars at Winchell's table—though he wasn't exactly a power broker—was Swifty Morgan, immortalized by Damon Runyon in "The Lemon Drop Kid." Swifty didn't drink or smoke, but he always sucked on lemon drops.

There are a hundred Swifty Morgan stories. He was a legendary con man, always looking for the shortest route to a big score. He is supposed to have approached Winchell and J. Edgar Hoover in their box at the racetrack one afternoon, and tried to sell them a hot ring. Hoover studied the proffered bauble. "How much?"

"For you, Chief," says Swifty, "five hundred dollars."

"Five hundred dollars!" cries Hoover. "Are you crazy? I'll give you a hundred."

And Swifty says, "Why, there's a bigger *reward* out on it!"

He became my personal jeweler. I was saving money because I wanted to buy Jeanette a diamond, and Swifty said, "I got just the ring for you."

"Where is it?"

"See the guy at the bar? It's on his finger." (Old joke.)

My engagement to Jeanette wasn't as easy as I'm making it sound. She had been accepted to Brooklyn College, but I said, "Marry me or forget it. Because if you go to college, you'll never marry me, you'll be too smart."

She agreed to throw in her lot with me, and I went to see her mother and father. By this time they had resigned themselves to the fact that I was dating their daughter, but they thought college would change all that; at college, she'd meet a nice boy. (They had a guy named Heshy picked out; he became a dentist. Years later he came lumbering backstage after a show of mine—he weighed 300 pounds— and I was standing there in my silk tuxedo and I looked at Jeanette and she said, warningly, "Don't you say a word.")

To Mr. Sprung, it was clear I was not a nice boy. We had a scream- ing confrontation in the Sprung apartment, with my future father-in- law providing the screams. "How could you do this to an innocent young girl who has her life in front of her? What are you? An *actor!*" I tried to back away from his fury and sat down on an antique chair and broke it. The very first time I'd ever been allowed past the Sprungs' front door.

Everything I did was wrong, to hear the Sprungs tell it, and poor Jeanette had to stand there and listen to the indictment. Finally I found my voice. It was very dramatic, my Bogart moment. I turned to Jeanette and said, "I don't know what I can promise you except one thing—it'll never be dull." To this day, every time something crazy happens, my wife says, "You told me."

We became engaged at a club called Queens Terrace (on 69th Street and Roosevelt Avenue) where I was working. In those days you could stay for a long time in a neighborhood club, if the neighborhood people liked you. I was at Queens Terrace for a year, and I followed Jackie Gleason, who had been there for *two* years. Every comic started in a local joint, and went on from there.

It's like when I was starting to move, some guy would tell some other guy, "Hey, there's a hot comic at Queens Terrace," and it was only ten minutes across the 59th Street Bridge, so every once in a while they'd bring an agent over, or a club owner. Because you were making some noise. Not like television where you get hot overnight, but there was a grapevine.

Like all the clubs, Queens Terrace was full of gangsters, and they liked me because I was funny. From my very early years, I was around the mob; they frequented—and often owned—the places where I worked. I found them fascinating, maybe because I had a lot of wise guy in me. I can still do a very impressive shoulder roll.

At Queens Terrace, the gentlemen of respect used to sit in the back and play cards. Frank Costello was referred to as Mr. C., Joe Adonis was Joey A., and there was Three-Finger Brown (his real name was Luchese), and a whole bunch of others. I used to come kibitz with them between shows. One time, there was a pretty young girl there, and Joey A. said, "Hey, Alan, say hello to my daughter."

I'm naive, what do I know. Six months later, I'm doing a benefit at the Latin Quarter and Joey A. is sitting there with his wife, and I walk over to pay my respects. And I say, "Oh, Mrs. Adonis, I met your beautiful daughter," and Mrs. Adonis says, "My beautiful who?" Guys had been killed for less. I learned a great lesson that night. If you don't want to have your throat cut, don't open your mouth.

4 ✑ DEAN

And ale we drank and songs we sung.

—CHARLES HENRY WEBB

WHEN I WAS living at the Bryant Hotel I was seventeen, eighteen, and my companions were all ten or twelve years older. I talk about that period now, and people say, "You must be eighty."

I remember the day Sonny King, one of our roommates, took a bride; he was the only guy who ever got married in Lindy's. And I remember the day Henny Nadel took a Brody. Just went up to the roof of the Bryant and jumped. It was devastating to us. We didn't know many junkies—we thought the only people smoking marijuana and taking dope were musicians—but poor Henny was ahead of his time; he went down with a crash, taking his demons with him.

Most of all, I remember Dean Martin, who was the biggest character in the group. I'd met him earlier, when I was working at Leon and Eddie's. He was struggling, but you wouldn't have known it because Dean never looked like he was struggling. He used to come in on Celebrity Night; every Sunday he'd get up and do a Bing Crosby takeoff. "Well, I'm packin' my grip and I'm movin' today—"

He was already twenty-nine, thirty, a grown man. He'd been a boxer, blackjack dealer, he was a rounder and a roustabout. The comedian Lou Costello had discovered him in a gambling joint in Covington, Kentucky, and brought him to New York. Lou Costello and Lou Perry were *paesans*, and Costello said to Perry, "Take care of Dean."

It was Costello who paid for Dean's nose job, to turn him into a matinee idol (before that, Dean had a nose that started on Times Square, made a right turn on 40th Street, then went south). I think he'd have made good anyway. I was crazy about him, he never treated me as a kid, but I learned never to leave any money on the dresser, because if he got up first, he'd take it.

He was the midnight burglar. You'd have to go to sleep with your cash in your socks. But Dean was a big sport; if you were tapped out, he'd lend you your own money back.

He was also the midnight prowler. Any unfortunate who had to sleep in the tub had to sleep with one eye open because Dean would get up to take a leak, and he'd turn on the bathtub faucets.

He and I used to hang out a lot at the Havana Madrid, a club owned by Angel Lopez, who was quite a famous Cuban impresario. (He also owned fighters, among them Kid Gavilan.) The Havana Madrid was on Broadway, right next door to the Winter Garden, and featured a lot of Latin acts.

But every once in a while, Angel Lopez would put in an American act, because he was trying to make it a crossover place, and that was how Lou Perry managed to book both Dean and me into the Havana Madrid.

Dean was headlining. He wasn't yet a star, but he'd already worked the Rio Bamba, the Martinique, all those clubs with Latin music, Latin decor, Latin acts. Everybody was doing the rumba, there were palm trees all over. Angel Lopez used to star Miguelito Valdez, Pupi Campo, Diosa Costello, Desi Arnaz, and now he was presenting Dean Martin. And as extra added attraction, Alan King.

Unfortunately, that booking took place during some kind of Latin convention. It was the wrong room for me; *nobody* in the audience spoke English. Dean sang—the language didn't matter, music is universal—but I was telling my cockamamie jokes, and I couldn't get a laugh.

I lasted one week. Dean was kept on, and I was replaced by a slick-haired kid doing a record act. Jerry Lewis would put a mop on his head and lip-synch an aria from *The Barber of Seville*. He was crazy even then. (I knew Jerry; I'd worked for his father, Danny Lewis, in the mountains. Danny was a Jolson impersonator, a handsome man, with an ego bigger than Jerry's, and his wife played piano for him.)

Anyway, the revue continued without me. The opening act was called Los Barancas. I'll never forget it, they did a wild exotic dance. She was brown-skinned, he was a Latin with a mustache, the Cesar Romero type, and the number was kind of Afro-Cuban, with drums. For their big finale they brought a pot of fire onstage (they had a little Sterno can that was lighted), and she would dance over it.

That was all Jerry Lewis needed. While Dean was singing, Jerry came out with this pot of fire and *he* danced over it, miming the agony of crotch burning. Dean continued to sing, and the audience had hysterics.

Dean always liked to do shtick with whatever comedian was on the bill with him. When we worked together, I'd wind up my act, Dean would come on and start a song, and in the middle of it, I'd wander out in my bathrobe, walk across the stage, and interrupt him to say, "Excuse me, what did you do with the soap?"

It brought the house down. But with Jerry, Dean went further, they went someplace neither one of them could have got to on his own. Dean left Lou Perry and signed with an agent named Abby Greshler, the palest man in the world (Milton Berle once joked that Abby was late for dinner because they'd sent him out to be colorized), and it was Abby who booked Martin and Lewis into the 500 Club in Atlantic City. That's where they made their big breakthrough. Next came the Copa, and Jerry stopped doing the record act and just did his craziness.

I've said this before, I've been watching comedy for over fifty years. I guess I've seen every comedy act, big and small, in the world. And nobody did what Martin and Lewis did to an audience. I mean, people laughed so hard they turned over tables and knocked down chairs. I'm talking about delirium.

Now they became big movie stars. They opened at the Paramount, and there were cops on horseback in the street to manage the crowds. I went backstage to see Dean, and we were looking out the window at these mobs, thousands of people, and Dean just stood there, shaking his head in wonder.

Let me digress briefly and jump ahead a few years for a Jerry Lewis story. By this time I too was a headliner, and I was set to open in Philadelphia at the Latin Casino, which was owned by a guy named Harry Steinman. One day Jerry Lewis called me and asked if I would put his father, Danny, the Jolson impersonator, on the bill. "You're the star," he said, "you can choose your opening act."

"Jerry," I said, "all you have to do is pick up the phone and say, 'Steinman, put my father in,' and it's a done deal."

So Danny Lewis was booked, and on opening night, he started getting hundreds of telegrams. "Kill 'em. Winston Churchill." "They ain't heard nothin' yet. Al Jolson." "Be good. Albert Schweitzer." Obviously, Jerry was sending his old man all these telegrams, and we're just getting ready to do the first show when Danny Lewis walks over to me with a tear in his eye and says, "Could you believe it? Jolie remembered."

People say Dean and Jerry wound up hating each other, it isn't true. They didn't hate each other, they lived different lives. Jerry was the single most ambitious man of all time, and Dean—what did Dean care? When Martin and Lewis split up, everybody said Dean Martin was just a singer, Jerry had the talent. But Jerry knew better.

Years later I interviewed him for a series called *Inside the Comedy Mind*, and on that show he called Dean "the finest actor that ever lived. . . . See, what Dean had is what George Burns honed for fifty years. Dean was born with it . . . a sense of breathing time. I could turn my head away and Dean would feel, in a breath, when I'd be back at him. . . .

"What Dean and I had, and we knew it, was this love affair. He loved this kid, the kid character. . . . My feeling for him was brother, was father, was hero. He was my Schwarzenegger, this handsome man whom the women went crazy for."

I reminded him that theirs had been the biggest breakup in the history of show business, and he came right back at me with the date they'd parted. "July 25, 1956." They'd been together since 1946. "We had a ten-year marriage," Jerry said, "and a honeymoon for the better part of eight and a half years.

"And then we invited some people to the honeymoon. That's what happened. Wives, outside interests, lawyers, friends. Friends are the most dangerous; strangers can't get close enough, but watch out for friends."

In the end, Jerry had to confess he couldn't blame friends, wives, or anyone else for the breakup. He wanted to direct, but Dean wasn't interested in Jerry's aspirations. "He believed," Jerry told me, "that what we had was what we should have lived with. And when I started to feel the need for growth, I made it very apparent to him. So I was really the reason that the split happened, I was responsible for it."

Of course, there was life for Dean after Martin and Lewis. He went on to make hugely successful movies, and he was also a hugely successful singing star with his own television show. He made a fortune, and when he got all this money, he started doing what he wanted to do. He played golf and got drunk and watched cowboy movies. He was a vagabond with a sense of comedy that was remarkable. He may have been the best straight man who ever lived, but he was never just a straight man.

My own feeling—despite Jerry's talking about how much they loved each other—is that Dean and Jerry were never friends, they were partners. I know a lot of show business acts where the curtain came down, and the partners went their separate ways.

Dean and I lost touch too, but when his son was killed in an airplane crash, I wrote him a long letter, and he answered. We shared a lot of memories. I have a picture in my office of him and me and Jerry and a beautiful girl singer named Maria Sanchez. Dean had a big thing with her at the Havana Madrid in 1947. It was just before I turned twenty, before anything sad or bad had happened to any of us, and in the picture, we're all grinning like idiots.

Maria Sanchez disappeared from our lives, and I seemed to hear less and less about Dean. I hadn't laid eyes on him in a long time, and then, a while ago (shortly before he died), I was in California, and somebody told me Dean went to a little Italian restaurant six nights a week and sat there drinking, all by himself. So I got in my car and went to that restaurant.

It was very dark in the place, and sure enough, there in a corner was Dean. I walked up behind him, and he knew somebody was standing there, but he probably thought it was an autograph hunter, and he didn't move. He just sat waiting for something to happen.

I reached over his shoulder and put a pad and pencil down in front of him. Without looking up, he said, "Who is this to?" I said, "Would you make it out 'To Maria Sanchez, a great lay,' and sign it, 'Love, Dean'?"

He yelped, and turned in his chair, and stretched his arms around my waist. "Maria Sanchez!" he said. He was laughing and crying and shaking.

I wanted to take him out of there, out of that dark corner, but nobody could ever take Dean anywhere he didn't want to go. I wanted us to be young again, and him to be standing in the sun, swinging a golf club.

I went back to my hotel thinking about him, my vagabond friend. He was a gambler, a drinker, a womanizer—all the good things. And that act, Martin and Lewis, was as funny as anything ever was or ever will be.

5 / THE WEDDING

*When you're a married man, Samivel, you'll understand a good
many things as you don't understand now; but vether it's worth
while goin' through so much to learn so little, as the charity-boy
said ven he got to the end of the alphabet, is a matter o' taste.*

—CHARLES DICKENS

I DIDN'T WANT a big wedding, but my father-in-law had to have a
big wedding, because he was so important in the neighborhood. It was
a matter of pride. If he was going to marry off his daughter, he was going to do it right. (Since I was marrying Sprung's daughter, everybody
thought that we didn't need any money, so we got fourteen menorahs
and eleven silver-bound prayer books.)

The ceremony took place in the East Midwood Jewish Center in
Brooklyn; it was a beautiful temple. My grandfather had never seen
anything like it, and he was walking around—he went upstairs, he
went downstairs—admiring everything, and he got lost.

Time is passing, I hear my mother, frantic, buttonholing relatives:
"Where is Grandpa? Where is *Zaide*? Where *is* he?" and I hear my
soon-to-be father-in-law overriding her: "We're going down the aisle
without him!" when all of a sudden an elevator door opens, and my
grandfather ambles out, zipping up his fly—"Such a fancy toilet," he

says—and steps right into the procession. Just as the music starts to play. We're going crazy, and he walks in like nothing happened. He was a riot.

So was my uncle Hymie, my mother's youngest brother. Hymie was probably the person who pointed me toward show business because he was the only member of the family who was born in this country, and he loved to go to vaudeville.

I called Hymie my drinking uncle, and I wasn't slandering him. Before my wedding, he was already bombed. In those days, there was a quiz show where the announcer would ask a contestant who had won, say, thirty-two dollars, "Will you take the thirty-two dollars or try for sixty-four dollars?" If the contestant elected to try and double his money, some clown in the audience would inevitably holler out, "You'll be *sah-ah-rry!*"

That's what Hymie did at the wedding. The rabbi was speaking in solemn tones—"Do you take this woman—" when my uncle Hymie stood up and yelled, "You'll be *sah-ah-rry!*"

It was a circus. I spent the evening playing the drums, everyone was drunk, and my friend Mac, in a top hat, was eating the centerpieces.

Our marriage went downhill from there. That first year my career slid into the toilet. The war was over, all the comedians who had been in the army were back home, and not only had I been working, but I'd been stealing their material, so I was wanted, dead or alive.

"You'll give up show business," my father-in-law said. "You'll come to work for me, you'll make a good living." And I said no thanks. "No way I'm going to work in the monument business."

But I was having a very tough time. Even my wife started saying, "You'll take a day job for a couple of months."

"Not me," I said. "Show business is my life."

A life that seemed to be destined for a pitiful end. I couldn't get work, and we had no money. I was so angry I used to come home and punch the refrigerator door. I finally broke it, pushed my hand right through it. Jeanette was frightened and depressed, she didn't know where we were heading, and we argued a great deal.

That summer we went to the mountains, to the Waldemere Hotel in Livingston Manor. It wasn't a honeymoon, I was working there. We had one room, with no closet. A pipe rack was suspended across the bed, and all our clothes had to hang from that pipe rack. We slept the whole summer with clothes tickling our chins every time we turned over. And a lot of the time, Jeanette sat in our room and cried. Here was this eighteen-year-old girl, just finished high school, gave up college, gave up everything—and for what? A room with no closets?

Back in Brooklyn, it wasn't much better. Our apartment on Bedford Avenue featured a bathroom that reminded me of our room in the mountains; instead of a pipe across the bed, there was a clothesline that ran across the toilet bowl. Water from wet underwear and silk stockings was always dripping right over the toilet seat. I used to go in there with a little umbrella, which Jeanette did not find amusing. "Could you give me your bathroom schedule, so I can wash out a few things?" she would say frostily.

Always I was chasing work, and sometimes I caught it. I got a one-week contract to play the Town Casino in Buffalo. It was a big club, a cavern with maybe a thousand seats.

And after the first night, I got fired by one of the owners, a man named Harry Altman. Furious and humiliated, I insisted he pay me in full. He said he would, but I'd have to come to the club every night and sit backstage for the entire week, even though I didn't go on.

Years later, I was a headliner, and I got another offer from the Town Casino. I told my beloved and beleaguered manager, Harry Adler, no. "I'll never work for Altman again."

He argued, "You're getting five thousand a week everywhere else? Let's ask for ten, that's the way to get even, take the money."

Harry Altman agreed—reluctantly—to pay the price, but I was still brooding. That man had made me sit for a solid week in a dressing room—through two shows a night—and even worse, he'd made me report on time. Now I was about to fill his club—opening night, both shows were sold out. After the first show, Altman came backstage to congratulate me. "You were great, I'll see you tomorrow."

I said, "What do you mean, you'll see me tomorrow?"

"I'm going home," he said.

"No," I said. "If you're not here for the second show, Harry, I'm not going on."

The second show wasn't till midnight, and he was really tired, but I'd been waiting a long time for revenge. He looked at me. "What does that mean? What are you talking about?" He really didn't remember our history, he must have fired so many people over the years.

My manager backed me up. "Mr. Altman, Alan wants you here for every show."

Harry Altman was confused. In the beginning, I think he must have believed I just liked him so much I wanted him around all the time. He didn't understand it, but out in the street, people were already lining up for the twelve o'clock show, and he was a businessman. He sat down on a chair in my dressing room.

I made him sit in that chair through both shows for the whole engagement. He should have been home in bed, we both knew it, and he finally asked, "What did I do to deserve this?"

"You fired me," I said. "And you made me sit here anyway, just to get my paycheck."

He swore on his children's lives he hadn't done it, he didn't remember it, but I was remorseless.

My second show didn't wind up until 2 A.M., and every morning, at two, he was in my dressing room.

My manager always said, "Don't get mad, get even."

I never *did* get even with Al Jolson. (How's *that* for name-dropping?) In Hollywood, in 1947, I was playing a small club called Billy Gray's, and Al Jolson came in one night and sat through my whole performance with his back to me. (When *The Jolson Story* came out in the movies, there was a big sign on Sunset Boulevard that bragged, "Jolson's Back!" "Right," I said to Jeanette. "I remember it very well.")

One night Celeste Holm came into Billy Gray's. She was then making *Gentleman's Agreement* at Fox, and she invited me to visit her on the set. I wanted to meet one of the picture's stars, John Garfield. He came from the Lower East Side, he'd been in the Group Theater, he was always playing a kid from the streets who was going to make it. I grew up doing an impression of him; mostly it consisted of saying, "Sure, sure, sure—"

He was a little guy, feisty, just like he was on the screen. Garfield, Cagney, all those great stars had that energy. Garfield told me a story about coming home to New York right after he'd finished making *Body and Soul*. "You always think you're bigger than you are," he said, "until somebody puts you back in your place."

He'd been visiting his old agent on Broadway and 48th Street, and he had to get to the East Side to meet someone for a drink. It was pouring rain, no cabs to be had, people huddling under theater marquees trying to stay dry. Being a New Yorker, Garfield figured he could duck into the subway and shuttle across town.

It was rush hour, five o'clock, so he raced down the subway stairs and onto a crowded train. Nobody paid any attention to him, except for one little old lady. She smiled, and he smiled back. At 42nd Street, he pushed his way out through a mass of sweating humanity and found the little old lady was following him.

He slowed down so she could catch up. "Excuse me," she said, "are you Julie Garfinkle?"

"Yes, ma'am," he said.

"Did you live on Eighth Street and Avenue B?"

"Yes."

"Your mother's name was Sarah?"

"Yes."

Triumphantly, the little old lady nodded. "I lived in the same building!"

"Oh," said Garfield, all movie star charm, "I'm so glad to see you."

"Tell me," said the little old lady, "vot are you doing now?"

I thought of that a long time afterward, when a similar thing happened to me. By then I was starring on *The Ed Sullivan Show*, and Ed had brought a whole troupe of us regulars to a CBS convention at the Palmer House in Chicago. Having entertained the conventioneers, and done well, I was standing in the lobby, surrounded by Sullivan and James Aubrey and all the other CBS big shots, and feeling very good about myself, when a guy walked by. He had one of those suitcases on wheels, like a jewelry salesman, and he yelled, "Hey, Kniberg!"

I recognized this guy from the old neighborhood.

"Hi," I said, "how are you?"

"What are you doing here?" he said.

"I'm here for a convention."

"What kind of convention?"

"A television convention."

"You in television?"

"Yeah."

"Wholesale or retail?" he said. And I'm standing there with the president of CBS.

I said, "Repairs, you asshole."

It was the Garfield story all over again, but this time I had the punch line.

My whole life, since I've been well known, people have been coming up to me and saying I looked like their brother or their husband. It still drives me crazy. One night in Las Vegas, I was finished with my second show, I had half a load on, and I was running through the crowd with two security guards, on my way up to the hotel room to change. And this woman grabs me by the hand and pulls me into the hall.

"I gotta tell you something," she says. "My husband, everywhere we go, they say, 'Alan King, Alan King, Alan King, Alan King.' " Now she starts yelling, "Seymour, come over here!" and here comes this guy with a broken face, weighs about 300 pounds, five foot four, I swear. And my wife says to the woman, "They *do* look alike."

Civilians say such funny things to performers. "I saw you one night in Seattle, you did a concert there, you weren't so good." Oh really? And I'm trying to get away, but the guy is still expressing himself. "I also saw you in Chicago one time, and you weren't a big hit that night either."

Or a man will say, "You went to school with my brother."

"Yeah? Where did your brother go to school?"

"In Middletown, New York."

I used to say, "Right, give him my best," but now I announce flatly, "I've never been to Middletown, New York."

Not that people take no for an answer. "First time I saw you was at the so-and-so theater in Maine."

"I was never there."

"Don't tell me you were never there, I *saw* you there."

"Don't *you* tell *me*, lady, I know every place I ever played in my life—" By now, the husband is pulling her away, and my wife is pulling me in the other direction.

Sometimes I get, "I never liked you, but my mother was crazy about you, can I have your autograph?" and I say, "Why don't you send your mother around?"

When Jeanette and I were first married, I was still doing an act that consisted of a little piece of Phil Foster, a little piece of Jerry Lester, a little piece of Milton Berle, but a comedian called Fat Jack E. Leonard changed all that.

Jack was a native of Chicago, he'd grown up with Mike Todd, another local boy who'd made good, and it was in Chicago that I really got to know him. I was playing in a revue at the State Lake Theater, and he was playing the Chicago Theater, and he let me hang out with him.

One day he told me about a guy who was appearing in the 5100 Club on Madison, a little bit beyond the Loop. I mean no one outside of Chicago had ever heard of this guy, but he was big there. So Fat Jack said, "After we do our last shows, we'll go see him."

We walked into the 5100 Club that night, and it was packed. We sat down and a guy with a big nose came out and started talking. He told stories about his family, he told stories in dialect, and there was no sense of hurry; we were watching somebody in complete control of what he was doing, and in complete control of his audience.

I'd been taught if they don't like one gag, go on to the next, it was all "But seriously folks," and then you'd fill in the holes, do a joke, do a cough, do *something*, because you had to keep going. If you're dying, talk louder and faster.

Now I'm sitting in the back of the 5100 Club watching this big-nosed comic, and he's telling a story about a guy whose car breaks down. And the guy opens up the trunk, and there's no jack, so he decides to walk in the rain to get help. The performer did it dramatically, he put on a hat, turned his coat collar up, and you got the feeling this was really a man with a flat tire walking in the rain on a deserted road and searching for a gas station.

56

All the while he walked, he kept talking. "I'll ask him for a jack. I'll say, 'How much for a jack?' and he's gonna say, 'Ten dollars. Ten dollars for the jack.' And I'll say, 'Ten dollars for the jack? I don't want to *buy* the jack, I want to *borrow* the jack.' I'll offer him three dollars, and he'll say no—"

In character, he walked and talked, a guy building up a head of steam, until finally he reached the gas station, walked in, and said, "You can take your jack and shove it."

The comedian was Danny Thomas, and he was probably the greatest influence in my show business life. When I saw Danny Thomas, I knew what I had to do.

6 ∽ I Learn Some New Tricks

In spite of their self-centredness, actors are uncertain in their hearts, though they may appear boundlessly confident before an audience.

—SIR JOHN GIELGUD

THROUGHOUT WORLD WAR II, it had been let's have fun tonight, because tomorrow we may die, it was that whole raucous wartime behavior. But now the soldiers were home, starting families, looking for houses in the suburbs, and I thought even though Danny Thomas was angry and funny, there was personal stuff in his material, there was humanity.

It took a lot of guts; there was a lot of Danny he was exposing, and it made a huge impression on me, the way audiences identified with him.

I didn't say anything to anybody, not even Jeanette. It wasn't something where I went home and got out a typewriter, but it was marked in my brain.

Already I'd been reviewed in *Variety*, where the critic called me "a funny young man" but added, "Don't know how he'll do west of the Hudson." That had bothered me. I didn't want to be consigned to the Catskills for my working life.

But trying to be somebody I wasn't didn't prove successful either—Hemingway said, "Write what you know"—so I went back to my roots. And lived to discover that stories of my childhood were like Levy's rye bread, you didn't have to be Jewish to enjoy them.

About two years after I'd seen Danny Thomas in Chicago, I was working in Miami, and I took part in a benefit at the Lord Tarleton Hotel, owned in part by Al Jolson. (There was a room in it called the Jolson Room; leave it to Jolson to name a room after himself.)

All the comedians had turned out for this benefit, Jackie Miles, Steve ("A Fool and His Fiddle") Murray, Jerry Lester, Monroe Seaton, Dean Murphy, Fat Jack E. Leonard, the hot comics of fifty years ago.

And every one of them did a bit, but not his regular act—you did your regular act for civilians—so there were surprises. The whole idea was to see who could ad-lib the best. When my turn came, being a newlywed, I got up and started talking about my wife. Not like Henny Youngman—"Take my wife, please," or "My wife is so ugly that . . . ," or "My wife is so cheap . . ."—but in a dramatic sense. I acted out a little play, I became all the characters.

When I came back to the table, Jack E. Leonard said, "That's it. That's what you're going to do from now on, no more one-liners."

I began basing my stories on who I was, what I was, what I wanted to be. When I developed a routine about "my brother, the doctor," it worked because I made it personal. "My brother is the youngest member of the College of Physicians and Surgeons," I'd say. "And I wouldn't let him cut my nails." A routine about doctors in general wouldn't have had the same impact. As long as I was making fun of *my* brother, I could go as far as I liked.

In the fullness of time, I broadened my attacks to include airlines, life in the suburbs, insurance companies. I would tell about not being able to collect on a fire and theft insurance policy after my house was robbed. "They said I should have had fire *or* theft, not fire *and* theft."

A devotee of other comedians, I watched everybody work. I watched the nightclub stars, and I watched the big stage comedians, Frank Fay, Jimmy Savo, Bobby Clark, and my all-time favorite, Bert Lahr. I went to school to them.

Lahr was a man of massive comedic talents but no formal education. I saw him and Tom Ewell in *Waiting for Godot,* went back to compliment Lahr on his performance, and said how wonderful the play was.

"Good," he said. "Maybe you can explain it to me."

Fred Allen was another early idol. He had his office in the Park Central Hotel, and he used to have lunch every day at the Stage Delicatessen with his writers, among them the legendary Goodman Ace and Nat Hiken (creator of *Sergeant Bilko* and *Car 54, Where Are You?*). Fred once said to me, "In order to get better, you've got to get smarter."

He was brilliant; he was, as they say, too good for the room. We don't have wits like Fred Allen anymore, that was another time and another place.

The straight plays I saw affected me too. I saw Frank Fay in *Harvey*, Kim Stanley in *Picnic*, and Laurette Taylor in *The Glass Menagerie*. I saw Lee J. Cobb in *Death of a Salesman*, and was destroyed. It was my father onstage, I couldn't get out of my seat. I was staggered by Marlon Brando in *A Streetcar Named Desire*. When he came on, the walls rumbled. For me, the watching was a learning process.

I saw the great ones, but I was lucky; I was never great. (Though I was always pretty damn good. "When you live in a world that is mediocre," my father said, "good is going to take you a long way.")

My theory is that people who are great have to follow their genius, and it goes anywhere it wants to go, they can't stop it, they can't channel it, it's an explosion. Einstein couldn't have stopped being Einstein if he tried. It was different for me, I was my own driving force, it wasn't my talent goading me.

It's like my success is my own little joke on everybody. I know something they don't know—they don't know how I did it. The secret is, it doesn't take much to be successful, it's the need to be somebody that matters. Genius is not required for comedy. Except maybe in the case of Charlie Chaplin.

Among my comedy mentors were Jack Benny and Joe E. Lewis. As I've already said, Danny Thomas and Milton Berle made contributions to my craft, but Jack Benny and Joe E. Lewis made contributions to my life.

Joe E. was a saloon comic, a rough kind of guy, and Jack was so dainty, and I loved them both. They were the kindest men I ever knew.

Neither of them ever said a bad word about anybody. If you'd mentioned Hitler to Joe E., he'd have said, "So, he made a few mistakes." And Jack thought everything was the greatest. Every cup of coffee was the greatest cup of coffee, every cigar the greatest cigar. Once when we were drying off in a health club, he told me, "These are the greatest towels I ever used."

Joe E., of course, wasn't well known outside of nightclubs. The New York season would start in September, when he opened at the Copa. I thought of him as a father figure till the day he died. Some father figure, he was America's favorite drunk, but he was a great man.

When I was very young, to supplement my income, I wrote one-liners for him—he paid me twenty-five dollars a page. Much later, after Sinatra played Joe E. in *The Joker Is Wild*—a picture in which Frank was surrounded with pretty women—I gave Joe E. a joke to use at the Copa. He would come out and tell the audience, "I went to see *The Joker Is Wild*. And I realized that Frank Sinatra had more fun playing my life than I had living it."

In 1949, I was appearing at the Paramount (the last of the big New York movie houses that still featured vaudeville) on a bill with Billy Eckstine, when I got a call from Joe E. He needed a favor. He was stuck in Chicago and couldn't get home in time to do a benefit that night. "Can you make an appearance for charity?" he asked me. "It's right across the street, at the Astor Hotel, you're four steps away."

I'd never turn Joe E. down, but it was a Saturday; we did six shows at the Paramount on Saturday, so I was not in the best frame of mind to do a benefit.

I came offstage, walked across the street to the Astor Ballroom, and said to the stage manager, "Listen, I've got an hour and a half between shows. If I don't go on now, I can't go on at all." So the bandleader interrupts the dinner: "Ladies and gentlemen, direct from the Paramount Theater, Alan King!"

I do half an hour and go back to my dressing room at the Paramount. The phone rings. It's Joe E. "What the hell happened? Where were you?"

"What do you mean, where was I? I just did half an hour in the Astor Ballroom."

"Schmuck!" Joe E. yells. "It was the Astor Roof!" I'd done half an hour in the wrong room.

I toured incessantly, opening for great singers—Lena Horne, Nat King Cole, Patti Page—but it was Tony Martin who gave my career a jump start. He was a major singing star, and he'd helped a lot of young comedians. He'd helped Sid Caesar, Jack Carter, Fat Jack E. Leonard, and after them, me. Everywhere he went, he insisted on having me open for him. He had the juice, he could do it.

Tony got me my first thousand-dollar week at the Flamingo Hotel in Las Vegas, in 1948. Those were the Ben Siegel days, the days when everybody I worked for got killed. Maybe I was a jinx. Right after that engagement, Ben Siegel was killed. Then I worked for Gus Greenbaum, and *he* got killed. Later on, books like *The Green Felt Jungle* were written about Siegel, Greenbaum, Henry Berman, all those guys. This one was a murderer, that one was affectionately called Ice-Pick Willie—my God, I thought, they'd been like uncles to me.

Ben Siegel gave me the name Shadow, because wherever Tony Martin was, I was right behind him. When I arrived in Las Vegas, it was a small town in the desert. There were three hotels, El Rancho Vegas and the Last Frontier, which were divorce havens, and a country-western place called the Thunderbird, and Benny Siegel had just built the Flamingo.

I remember standing with him in front of the Flamingo, wind blowing, sand blowing, sagebrush blowing, literally nothing there but that little highway that ran through the town, and he said, "Shadow, someday there'll be twenty hotels on this strip. It'll be the entertainment mecca of the world." And I said to myself, No wonder they call him Bugsy.

Among other things, he was a visionary. I saw Las Vegas grow. And we had so much fun, the performers, the acts from all the different places. We hung out together, and we never went to sleep until the sun came up.

For my opening there with Tony, I bought my first custom-made tuxedo. I'd loved clothes since I was a kid. I remember Pittsburgh Phil Strauss from Murder, Incorporated, who died in the electric chair. He used to hang out in my neighborhood, wearing this big tan George

Raft polo coat, and the first coat I ever bought myself was a tan polo coat.

Tony Martin loved clothes too. He was the best-dressed man I ever saw; he spent every afternoon shopping. I used to do a joke about him. I'd say, "Tony Martin and I went window-shopping, and he bought eight windows." One night, two weeks into our engagement—I was scheduled to do twenty minutes and get off so the star could come on—I was feeling my oats, so I stayed onstage ten minutes longer than I was supposed to. And in the wings, I could hear Tony clearing his throat. He wasn't happy with me, and after the show, he told me so.

Ben Siegel saw me looking gloomy and asked why. "Ah," I said, "Tony's giving me a hard time."

"Fuck Tony," says Ben. "I'm the boss, stay on as long as you want."

So the next night, I stayed on too long again, and when I came off, I hung up my precious tuxedo to dry, because the sleeves were wet with perspiration. But Tony got even. After I'd gone home, he went into my dressing room, tied the tuxedo's sleeves into a knot, and left them hanging that way.

Next day, I went crazy. I got an iron from the wardrobe mistress, and as I walked past Tony's dressing room, I stuck my head inside. "Tony, if you ever touch my clothes again, I'll kill you."

That night I stayed on even longer, and when I came back the following day, my tuxedo was in knots again. So while Tony was onstage, I took a big scissors and cut the sleeves off *six* of his tuxedos. At the elbows. Then I hid out till the next show.

I went downtown, and when I got back, the word was out. Tony was looking for me. He finally found me, and smoke was coming out of his ears. "You cut the sleeves off my tuxedos! You cut the sleeves off my tuxedos!" He was screaming like a banshee, everybody backstage was stunned by the noise, and then, suddenly, he started laughing. "You're fucking crazy," he said, and the tears were rolling down his cheeks.

We became brothers. When I worked in California, I'd stay at his house (it wasn't too bad sleeping under the same roof as Cyd

Charisse), and I wound up at parties where I had no right to be. I was mingling with the likes of George Raft, Peter Lorre, Harry James and Betty Grable, Phil Harris and Alice Faye (who had been Tony's first wife), Leo Durocher and Laraine Day, Humphrey Bogart and Lauren Bacall.

Tony headlined all over the country, and I went with him. Once, at the Chez Paree in Chicago, I finished my act and walked into the wings, and Tony was standing there with a fire bucket full of water, and he threw it at me. I came out to take my bow soaking wet. I didn't say a word, but three or four nights later, in the dark, as he's ready to go on, I call "Tony!" he turns around, and I hit *him* with a pail of water. Not at the *end* of his act but at the *beginning*. A showman to the quick, he said, "Ladies and gentlemen, I'm doing a tribute to Esther Williams."

Because I was out in Holmby Hills hanging around with Tony's friends, I met the producer Joe Pasternak, who was putting together a picture called *Hit the Deck,* a remake of an earlier MGM musical. Everybody and his brother was in that Pasternak movie; they used all the contract players on the lot. Tony Martin, Jane Powell, Ann Miller, Debbie Reynolds, Walter Pidgeon, Gene Raymond, they were all in it.

Pasternak was famous for telling everyone he met, "You're in my next picture," so when he said it to me, Tony warned, "Don't take him seriously."

But sure enough, there were two shore patrols in the movie, and Pasternak hired me and Henry Slate (one of the Slate Brothers) to play them. Henry and his brother ran a nightclub—it was a comedy club before there were comedy clubs—and Henry had done bit parts in pictures, and he and I had four scenes together. It was fun, but I didn't take it too big, I figured that was the beginning—and the end— of my movie career.

It wasn't. I get a call for a picture called *Miracle in the Rain,* written by Ben Hecht. The producer, Frank Rosenberg, wanted me to play the best friend of Van Johnson and Jane Wyman. Not only that, they were going to shoot in New York, in Central Park.

I showed up for the first day's work, and met Frank Rosenberg, and I knew something was wrong, but I couldn't put my finger on what it was.

Later, I found out that Rosenberg had wanted Henry Slate for the part. Somebody had shown him *Hit the Deck*—the scenes Henry and I had done together—and he'd thought he was okaying Henry.

At this time, my grandfather, to whom Alan King was one word—"Say hello to my grandson, Alanking"—was very ill. I went to see him in the nursing home, and he spoke to me in Yiddish. (When we were small, the grownups spoke Yiddish so we wouldn't know what they were talking about, which meant we all learned Yiddish. Then they had to start talking Polish and Russian.)

There was a shortage of wheelchairs in the nursing home, and when I left my grandfather, I went to a surgical supply store and ordered a brand new shiny aluminum wheelchair. I had the store put a tag on it that read "Harry Solomon."

Then I traveled back to California to finish *Miracle in the Rain*. My mother would report to me by phone. "You're not gonna believe what's going on with that wheelchair. First of all, everybody has to know that his grandson Alanking gave it to him, and at night, he covers it with a bedsheet, like a car."

While I was away, my grandfather had a stroke and was totally paralyzed. I called my mother every couple of days and she kept saying, "He's hanging in there." (He did hang in. Next time I saw him, he'd regained a little bit of his speech, and he showed me he could move one hand. Rabbi Solomon, who'd lifted heavy garbage cans and scared little children—in his decline, he was still a man to deal with.)

Despite Frank Rosenberg's having hired the wrong actor, I was pretty good in *Miracle in the Rain*, and I was offered a contract at Warner Brothers. I was making a thousand, fifteen hundred dollars a week in nightclubs, but I wanted to be a movie star. I signed for five hundred dollars a week.

One night—it must have been on a weekend, when we didn't have to get up early the next day—Jane Wyman took me to a big Hollywood party. And in comes Jack Warner, late and by himself. Everybody's around the piano singing, and Jack Warner loved to sing. He told bad jokes, and sang terribly, but he was a total vaudeville maven. He would rather have been Al Jolson than the head of Warner Brothers Pictures.

When I was a kid, I'd done Jolson impersonations; now Jack Warner and I are singing duets, and he's having the best time ever. He doesn't know me, but he figures I must be somebody, or what am I doing in this house filled with celebrities? So he says to me, "Come on, there's a party up in Bel Air."

He had a Bentley convertible, and we drove to Bel Air and went through an electric gate, and once in the house, we did our vaudeville act again. We just went on the road; he took me to parties to sing with him. (During this time, he never knew I was making a movie at his studio.)

In 1955, I was back in Las Vegas headlining at the Flamingo, when I met Rosalind Russell. She was staying at the hotel doing a movie called *The Girl Rush*, about a woman who inherits a casino. Almost every night she came in to see my show. She told me the writers on her picture didn't really understand the language or the rhythm of Las Vegas. It ended up with her hiring me to write additional dialogue.

Roz had never shot craps, and one night she asked me to teach her how. We put in $500 each, and we won $26,000—she had $13,000, and I had $13,000. "Look how easy it is!" she was screaming.

After she went to bed, I lost $90,000. At 6 A.M., when Roz came out to wait in front of the hotel for the car to pick her up and take her on location, I was still standing around in my tuxedo. "Well," I said, "we had a big night. You won thirteen, and I lost ninety." She felt so bad. I'd been trying to stop gambling, but she didn't know that.

I was a bad gambler in those days. Everywhere I went, they'd say, Cut him off, no more money for King. My wife was back East in Rockville Centre—by now we had two kids running around in diapers—and I'd become a high roller. Jeanette never even knew I gambled until one day Walter Winchell wrote in his column that the three biggest losers in Las Vegas were Harry Belafonte, Phil Silvers, and Alan King. If she didn't leave me then, she was never going to leave me.

My marriage may be the only decision I made in my life that I never regretted. No matter how crazy I was, I always came home.

And home was New York. I didn't want to live on the West Coast. For me, it's too much sun, it's El Paso with movie studios, everything all stucco and white and hot and the buildings so small.

All my friends traveled west, chasing their careers, because that's where the business went. I'd go to a Hollywood party, and someone would always ask, "When are you moving out here?" I'd say, "You know, I was in Cleveland two nights ago, and I went to a party, and not one person there asked me when I was moving to Cleveland."

The Academy Award–winning director Joe Mankiewicz was a great writer, and when I'd got to know him in New York, he'd been a great raconteur. But when I met him again in Beverly Hills, the first thing he said to me was, "How about this weather?"

"Come on, Joe," I said, "everywhere I go out here, they say, 'How about this weather?' but I expect more from Joe Mankiewicz."

He grinned. "I've been here so long, I've succumbed."

Jeanette wasn't crazy about California, either (now she's grown to love it because of the friends, the tennis, the golf), but she'd have made it work anywhere I settled. I was the one who refused to live there.

Once in the early fifties—I had a job on the West Coast—I transplanted Jeanette and our infant son, Bobby, to a kind of motel apartment in Westwood. It was terrible, with a tiny kitchen; I can still smell the wallpaper, the mustiness of it.

So we came back to our twenty-five-thousand-dollar tract house on Long Island, but I was away so much, and there was a price to pay for that. When Bobby was very young, he was asked in school to write a page about his father, and he wrote, "Everybody likes my father, they laugh at him, and he sleeps a lot."

Because I was always coming in from the road, or from a club, and it would be five in the morning when I'd get home, Jeanette spent those early years going, "Shh, Daddy's sleeping."

It wasn't that I was a bad father, I just wasn't there, so my wife had to raise the kids. I've tried to make up for it, and I've done a pretty good job. I have a pretty good relationship with my children. Still, if I had it to do over, I'd do it different. I'd pack the kids in the car and go, and they'd be in Pittsburgh with me when I was in Pittsburgh. Not then, though; then we thought kids had to go to the right schools.

Oh yeah, you pay for that. And your kids pay for it, but I didn't know it then. And if you had told me, I wouldn't have believed you, because in 1956, something happened that convinced me life could not get any better.

7 ⌘ HEY, JUDE

Here a star, and there a star,
Some lose their way.

—EMILY DICKINSON

IN 1956 I was invited to work with Judy Garland, who was about to open at New York's Palace Theater in one of her many comebacks.

The first half of the bill would be variety, five different acts. Then a thirty-minute interval. Then Judy would do her turn.

Even though I didn't know her or her then husband and manager, Sid Luft, I said yes, absolutely. Judy was a legend, and I would be on Broadway, which, to a New York actor, is the only place that counts. But I made one condition. I had to be the act to close the first half of the show.

Everything was agreed to, contracts were signed.

Now there's an act called Kovach and Robovsky on the bill. They're adagio dancers, and they're on their way back here from Europe when the boat—it was the *Andrea Doria*—sinks. They survive, make headlines, get a lot of publicity. So when I show up at the Palace for the first rehearsal, I look at the board where the running order for the show is posted, and there it is, Kovach and Robovsky are closing the first half.

My long-suffering manager, Harry Adler, is with me, and I say, "Come on, Harry, let's go," and I turn and walk out of the theater.

As yet I haven't met Judy or Sid Luft, and now I don't *want* to meet them. Sol Schwartz, the president of RKO (which owned the Palace), and Larry Barnett, my agent at MCA (head of the Band and Act Department), are by then chasing me and Harry Adler down Broadway, traveling south from 48th Street, and one of them is yelling, "Alan, you're crazy!"

"I'm not going on," I yell back. "I have a contract that says I close the first act."

I'm so angry my actor's ego has completely taken over. I'm thinking, What do I need this for? What do I need Judy Garland for? Kovach and Robovsky survived the *Andrea Doria,* so they're gonna close the first act? And here's the president of RKO, and one of the top guys at MCA, chasing me, and my poor manager isn't saying a word, and I just keep moving and hollering, "I'm not coming back."

When I finally stop, they're right at my heels, and Sol says, "Alan, just go out there and kill the people. Kovach and Robovsky won't be able to follow you." Still livid, I come back with them to the Palace. "I'll do it opening night," I say, "and then it has to change."

So the three of them beard Sid Luft backstage, but he's adamant. "Nobody tells me how to produce my show! Alan King will go on when I tell him to go on, next to closing in the first act! Kovach and Robovsky are closing the act!"

I start toward the stairs. My dressing room is on the third floor, no elevator, and on my way, I pass Miss Garland's dressing room. The door is closed, and I know she must have heard all the commotion, but she still hasn't shown herself. To me, anyway.

Opening night, I'm seething, three flights up. Over the backstage speakers, I can hear the first three acts, and then it's time for me, and I slog down, walk out on the stage, and it's an all-star audience. A Judy Garland opening at the Palace, you just can't imagine who's there.

And I'm so filled with rage I go out and beat this audience to death. I stop the show cold, take a bow, and walk off. And here come

Kovach and Robovsky tripping on with their dance to "Clair de Lune" or something, and I run up those stairs, and instead of being elated, I'm still mad.

Barry Gray, an old friend—he's had a talk show on radio for years and years and years—doesn't even wait for Kovach and Robovsky to finish, he races back to congratulate me, and we're talking, and suddenly there's a knock on my dressing room door. I open it, and here's this little tiny woman in a grubby terry cloth robe with greasepaint stains all over the collar. She's all made up for the stage, and she says, "Young man, you can close my fucking first act anytime you like," and then she turns around and goes back downstairs.

That was the first time I ever met Judy Garland.

From that night on, I closed the act.

Judy and I worked together for years. We played twenty-six weeks at the Palace, and then we toured the country. People would ask me, "How come you stayed with her so long?" and my joke was, "Because nobody could make the speech, 'Miss Garland will not appear tonight,' better than I could."

Judy loved that; she had a laugh like a horse. She was a great, incredible woman, but she could suck your blood. I used to come home drained, and my wife would say, "How can you do it?" Every night, it was like waiting for a hanging; we never knew what the hell was going to happen.

I've said it a thousand times, when she was good, she was the greatest thing that ever happened on a stage. And when she was bad, she was still pretty good.

She and I became inseparable, and when she'd have her breakdowns, it was terrible. She dreaded going onstage, she was so fearful, she used to shake before she went out.

Sunday nights at the Palace, all the big stars working on Broadway would come to see Judy. (The legitimate theaters were dark on Sunday.) Julie Andrews, who was starring in *My Fair Lady*, was there every Sunday night, which was more than you could say for Judy. Two or three times a week, I'd walk in the stage door and hear this screaming, and she'd be locked in her dressing room, and the stage manager would warn me, "She's not going on tonight."

I'd knock at her door, and I'd hear an ashtray crash against the wall. "Stay out of my life! Who is it?"

"Alan."

"Alan? You alone?"

"Yeah."

"Okay, come in." And she'd unlock the door.

She'd cry, the dressing room would be all broken up, and I never knew what it was about. She'd say, "Nobody believes me, Alan, I have laryngitis." It was psychosomatic, but to her it was laryngitis. I don't care what caused it, she had it.

At that time she was obese, and Norman Norell, the famous designer, had lined her gowns with corset steels, the better to squeeze her in; it was like singing in a suit of armor. But Norell was renowned for his beaded creations, and if you owned one, you thought you had to wear it forever.

I remember this particular Sunday night, Liza, who was maybe thirteen, was sitting in the audience with George Hamilton—she was crazy about George Hamilton—and I was locked in Judy's dressing room, with her whispering, "I can't go on."

It had become a tradition. I would sit with her and kibitz and try to get her ready. Not only did she suffer from stage fright, but she was also a naturally suspicious person. She thought she was being used by everybody, and a lot of the time she *was* being used; she used to call herself a piece of meat that sang.

That night I said, "Judy, the place is loaded with every star on Broadway, and I don't have to tell you rumors are rampant that you're back here drinking and doing drugs. So here's what we should do. Let me bring you out at the top of the second act, and you tell the audience, 'I'm sorry, I'm sick,' and at least they'll see that you're not falling down drunk or bouncing off the walls from drugs."

She had a pair of Chinese lounging pajamas, black with some red appliqué on them, and little Chinese slippers in which she used to greet guests after a performance, and I said, "Don't put on a gown. Put on that beautiful little Chinese jacket with the pants." The jacket covered her, so she didn't look too fat. She trusted me, I convinced her this was the way to go, and then I went out to talk to the audience.

"Miss Garland will not appear—" I began, and there was a roar of disappointment from the house, and I was trying to calm them down. "Ladies and gentlemen," I said, "she'd like to tell you herself." And I went to the wings to get Judy.

She was grabbing my hand so hard my knuckles were white, and everybody stood up and gave her an ovation. She looked like a little china doll, and they were all screaming, and she was trying to say something in a hoarse whisper, and she wouldn't let go of my hand.

After the first act, Liza had come backstage, and she was in the wings watching her mother apologize to the audience. I broke Judy's grip, left her standing there, went and got Liza, and brought her on. The place went wild.

Judy may have had no childhood herself, but she loved her kids, she was a great mother, and when Liza appeared, Judy looked down into the pit and said, "Okay, why don't we just try 'Toot Toot Tootsie'?" Every once in a while she would bring Liza on to do "Toot Toot Tootsie" with her, so she was comfortable with that, it was easy. And as they sang, I could heard her voice clearing. They did one more number, and then I walked on and led Liza away, and Judy did another hour and a half.

And she never wore a Norell gown again. Even when she got thin, she still preferred working in tops and pants. She said all of a sudden she had freedom. And the truth was, the people who came to her shows didn't care if she was fat or skinny, all they wanted was to see Judy.

On the nights when she wasn't having a problem, she could go out and have fun. I remember once we went to El Morocco, and she danced with this young senator from Massachusetts, and she came back and told me, "He's going to be president of the United States."

"A Catholic from Boston is going to be president of the United States?" I said. "Are you kidding?" (In later years, assorted Kennedys would show up wherever Judy played, that's how I got to know them.)

After the Palace, we trekked across the country. Was Judy shooting up? If she was, I never saw it. She drank, but she didn't do it in front of me, and the only reason I knew she took uppers and downers was because she told me so.

Even as a child, she'd been chunky, and MGM thought a movie star should be svelte, so she'd grown up with diet pills. ("You see that girl?" Louis B. Mayer is supposed to have said. "She used to be a hunchback. You see what I've made her into?") And even as a child, she'd been a poor sleeper, so she'd take sedatives to sleep, and then she'd be drugged in the morning and take stimulants to come alive again.

Another problem. Judy and Sid were always out of money. I don't know why. Somebody was always suing them, attaching their belongings, but they lived—forget about it—Judy lived like a star.

Anyway, that road tour was exhausting. Judy and I were the entire company. I did the first act, she did the second act, and at the end I came back, and together we did "A Couple of Swells," the duet in battered top hats and hobo clothes that Judy and Fred Astaire had made immortal. (She taught me that number on a Sunday in Chicago in the window of a Steinway piano store on Wabash Avenue; we worked around the clock to be ready to open Monday at the Orchestra Hall. Whether people liked me or not, they were going to have to admit it took guts for me to try to follow Fred Astaire.)

After Chicago, we played Detroit, we played San Francisco, we played Dallas. Nothing changed; Judy's appearances were sporadic, in and out. And since she could never sleep, she had a limousine on twenty-four-hour call to take her around the dark streets; the motion of the car soothed her. Eventually, I tried to stay at a different hotel from hers, because if Sid wasn't with her, she'd wake *me* in the middle of the night. The phone would ring: "Alan, let's talk."

Even when she was miserable, I could make her laugh. One night she called—we were in Detroit—and she was frantic. Sid had left for New York and she was alone. "I can't sleep, you've gotta come over."

I went over. She'd been drinking—it was one of the few times I ever saw her drink heavily—and we were talking, we'd been together a long time by now, and she looked at me and said, "How come you never made a pass at me?"

For once in my life I was speechless, I couldn't say a word.

She was really into the white wine, she'd had a couple of bottles by this time, and I pulled myself together. "Judy," I said, "for one fuck, do you want to wreck a friendship?" She looked at me, and started to laugh as only Judy could laugh.

We'd been working over a year and a half without a day off—literally—and we ended our tour at the Capitol Theater in Washington. Whereupon Judy announced that she was going to London to play the Dominion Theatre, a presentation house owned by the J. Arthur Rank Organization, and she wanted me to open for her.

"I can't go to England," I said. "They won't understand me, I'm a New York comic."

"They'll love you," she said.

I said no, I'd promised my wife a vacation, we were going to take six weeks and travel all over Europe. It would be our first trip abroad.

That September, Jeanette and I were in the Excelsior Hotel in Rome when the phone rang. In my mind's eye, I can still see the bed I was lying on. The call was from Sid Luft, in the States.

"Alan," he said, "I have your itinerary, and I need a very big favor. You know Judy is opening in London in November, and I know you're going to London, and you know the show inside out, so could you go see the Rank people at the theater and run the show down for them? Would you just do that so they could start to prepare?"

What could I say? Jeanette and I changed our plans a little bit and flew to London early. We got off the plane, and there was this big Daimler sent by the Rank Organization to pick us up. "Would you like to go to the hotel, or would you like to go to the theater?" a Rank representative said.

"I don't want to go to the theater now," I said. "I want to go to the Dorchester."

"Well," said the Rank man, "on our way, we have to pass by the theater."

"Fine," I said, "we'll see the theater." What did I care? So we drove down Tottenham Court Road, and there, in lights four stories high, it said JUDY GARLAND. And underneath that, it said ALAN KING. I have a picture of it.

I looked at this thing, and my hair stood on end. They had set me up. Then, more than half flattered, I started thinking about it. Nobody ever got billing above the title with Judy. Billing on the side, but never on the marquee. And there was my name with hers on the biggest sign you ever saw.

We got to the hotel and I phoned Sid Luft in New York. "You dirty so-and-so—" He was unrepentant. "Alan," he said, "she's not opening unless you open with her."

So now I started going around to theaters and clubs because I wanted to hear the comics, and I was totally confused. The comics were all cockney, the audiences were howling, and I couldn't understand a word.

Jeanette and I came home to the States, and I talked to everybody I knew who had played London. They said the English would understand me "because they invented the English language." I said, "What? Instead of suspenders, they say braces, instead of elevator, they say lift. Danny Kaye's a big star there, but Danny Kaye doesn't do jokes."

I was very concerned. I flew back to London without my wife, and resumed club hopping. I heard the English people laughing and I didn't know what they were laughing at; the cockney dialect might as well have been Chinese.

We opened, Judy and I, on a Sunday night, no master of ceremonies, nobody. We had Gordon Jenkins and his big sixty-piece orchestra in the pit, and Harry, my faithful manager (who in fact was London born), came over to hold my hand.

There was an overture, no introduction, and when I came on, nobody knew who the hell I was. Besides, there had been some screwup with the tickets, so in the first row, on the aisle, a woman who had been denied her seat was sitting on a man's lap. The woman was Lana Turner, and the man was the infamous Johnny Stompanato.

It was a black tie audience, and I thought, I can't go out there, what am I gonna do? Two Jews got off an Arab? What am I gonna do here?

The house lights went down, a spotlight picked me up, music started to play, and I walked on. There were 2,800, 3,000 people, however many the Dominion Theatre held, and four of them clapped. Even those four were only polite, not enthusiastic.

But I function well under that kind of pressure. When I get angry,

I'm better. And I was angry. I stood there doing my Jack Benny imitation, chin in my hand, staring out at the crowd. I just let 'em sit there. There was such a silence as you can't imagine. Finally, I said, "Right now, I'm not too crazy about you either."

Danny Kaye had found his way into the hearts of British audiences; he used to tell them their grass was greener. I thought about that, and also about a recent scandal. A female Member of Parliament had been standing on the corner of Curzon Street where the streetwalkers hung out, and some guy tried to pick her up, and she tried to get a law passed to remove streetwalkers from that corner.

So I ad-libbed. I looked around and said, "I know the grass is greener here because it never stops raining, and I also know that you are very friendly people. Because I was standing on the corner of Curzon Street, and five women tried to take me home with them."

The audience began to laugh. Judy was in the wings in that terry cloth robe, watching, and gradually, I got into my act. I didn't have to change one line. They understood everything, responded to everything, and when I ran off, Judy was waiting, jumping up and down, crying, "Go back, go back for another bow."

I went back and said, "You know, in America, we're taught that one of the great heroes of our Revolution was a silversmith named Paul Revere who got on a horse and raised the alarm throughout the countryside—"

You could have heard a pin drop as I went on. "And he shouted, 'The British are coming, the British are coming.' After the way you've received me tonight, the only thing I can tell you is that Paul Revere had a big mouth."

They stood up. They cheered.

We got tremendous reviews. Kenneth Tynan's was my favorite. Writing in *Punch*, he did four full pages about Judy's brilliance, and added two lines about me. "America's angry young man opened the first half," he said. "If a sawed-off shotgun could talk, it would sound like Alan King."

Judy was staying in the penthouse at the Westbury. It was the apartment of the man who owned the hotel; he'd turned it over to her. I was at the Dorchester, and she was still calling me in the middle of the night. She'd pick me up, we'd get into her damn limousine and drive around. Sometimes we'd go down to Curzon Street and gather hookers, four, five, six, every shape, every color, pack 'em in the car, go back to the Westbury, and she'd sit around talking to them till the sun came up.

Then she'd tell me, "Pay them," and I'd give each one a few pounds.

She just liked to hear the stories of their lives.

The following summer, she and I were among the entertainers invited to Glasgow, Scotland, to do a command performance for Queen Elizabeth and Prince Philip. Once I finished my turn (including the joke about how my wife was so neat that if I got up at night to go to the bathroom, when I came back, my bed was made, a story Prince Philip found "terribly amusing"), I went directly to my dressing room and started drinking. The scotch was good there; after all, the Scots invented it—probably right after the English invented the language— and I got bombed.

Everybody had to stand backstage for a reception line, and as the Queen moved down the line, the Lord Mayor of Glasgow made the introductions. "Your Majesty, Mr. King," he said.

The Queen said, "How do you do, Mr. King?" and I said, "How do you do, Mrs. Queen," and she stared at me, and then Prince Philip laughed. Thank *God* Prince Philip laughed.

In Glasgow, all of us performers were booked into the Central Hotel, right over the railroad station (from time to time the hotel rumbled so you'd think there was an earthquake), and Jeanette and I had a suite adjoining Judy's. The suites were identical, except that Judy's had a balcony.

That night, a crowd gathered in front of the hotel—there must have been a thousand people there—calling for Judy. Nobody had arranged it, it was spontaneous; it was like New Year's Eve.

Judy came out on her little balcony and, like the Pope, greeted her worshipful subjects, and they started to sing, "Will ye not come back again, me darling?" and everybody was crying. It was incredible. Judy melted. For some reason, she was able to be more lighthearted in Europe. At the end, she lived in England with that young rock 'n' roll fella she was married to. She seemed happy there.

A couple of years after Glasgow, I did another show with her. It was called *Judy at the Met,* and we played the old Metropolitan Opera House just before they tore it down. I was assigned to Robert Merrill's dressing room, and when I walked in, I found a message scrawled on the mirror. "Dear Alan," it said, "please don't pee in my sink. Bob."

John Bubbles, of the great vaudeville team Buck and Bubbles, was in the cast; he and Judy were going to do "Me and My Shadow" together. We went into rehearsal and discovered that Judy needed another five minutes for a particular costume change.

Now, this costume change came up in the second act. I'd already done my monologue in the first, but I had an idea. All my life I'd wanted to do a number with John Bubbles. George Gershwin wrote the character of Sportin' Life for him, and I knew every bit he'd ever done with Buck in the big floppy shoes.

I outlined my plan. John and I would both wear white tie and tails. I would come on and sing, "I always go to see a show so I can watch a song and dance man," and then John would strut out and dance around me, and we would do some of the old jokes he used to do with Buck.

I'd say, "John, I came by your house last night. You shoulda pulled down the window shades, I saw you kissing your wife." And he'd laugh, and I'd say, "Why are you laughing?" and he'd say, "I wasn't even *home* last night."

Then I'd say, "I saw you running yesterday, why were you running?" and he'd say, "I was running to stop a fight." "Who was fighting?" "Me and some other guy. You don't think my legs was gonna stand around and watch my body be *abused,* do you?"

We auditioned it for Judy, and she said, "Perfect"; it gave her the time she needed for her change. It was lovely, it was show business. And I got to share a stage with John Bubbles, that beautiful, talented man.

I also got sandbagged into going on the road again with the Garland traveling circus. Judy told me she and Sid thought I had a talent for producing; she said I paid attention, and they valued that. I was headlining on my own by then, but I couldn't turn them down, so Judy and Buck and I were off and running—to the Chicago Opera House, the San Francisco Opera House, the Dallas Opera House. It wasn't *Judy at the Met* anymore, it was *Judy at the Opera.*

79

When we played Chicago, Cary Grant, who was there making *North by Northwest*, came every night. I'd say, "Oh God, there he is again." Because you can listen to Judy Garland sing every night, but you can't listen to the same jokes every night. Still, Cary sat there roaring with laughter; he loved the entire show. Cary Grant laughing at my stories, and me dancing with John Bubbles. It was the most exciting time of my life.

After we finished the opera house circuit, I didn't see Judy for quite a while. She'd been living in England, she'd lost a lot of weight, and David Begelman and Freddie Fields brought her home to do Carnegie Hall. Jeanette and I were invited. We went, and found ourselves sitting next to Harold Arlen. When Judy came out and opened her mouth, Arlen murmured, "It's going to be fine."

Because anybody who knew her could tell. I'd never seen her look so beautiful, I'd never heard her sing so well. As always, she closed with "Over the Rainbow," and there was Arlen, the guy who wrote it, sitting right there, beaming. I turned to him and said, "You were right." The album *Judy at Carnegie Hall* was recorded that night.

At the party afterward, Judy was in high spirits; that was the last time I ever saw her.

She died in 1969. Liza made the arrangements for the funeral at Frank Campbell's in New York. And out in front, on Madison Avenue for about six blocks, there were police and wooden sawhorses to control the crowd, and all these limousines pulling up. Only eighty people had been invited to the chapel, and the invitations said no one would be admitted past twelve noon.

We sat down, and at twelve o'clock sharp, the doors were closed, and the service started. I tapped Liza on the shoulder—now she was a grown woman, and a star in her own right—and she and Sid Luft, who was sitting with her, looked around, and I said, "It's the first time Judy's ever been on time." And both Sidney and Liza started to laugh.

James Mason did the eulogy. He didn't know Judy very well, except that they had been together in *A Star Is Born*, but if you wanted somebody to do a eulogy, you'd ask James Mason. I mean, you couldn't get anybody better unless it was Winston Churchill. He was charming and touching and light, and the ceremony wasn't very long, maybe half an hour. When we came out of Campbell's and got into our car, my wife said to me, "Do you realize that you smiled through the entire service?"

And I said, "You know something? That's the way I remember Judy. Not the sadness, just the laughs."

Just the singing and dancing.

8 ∽ DR. JEKYLL AND
MR. KNIBERG

Some men, some men
Cannot pass a
Crap game.

—DOROTHY PARKER

WHEN I TAUGHT Roz Russell to shoot craps, I was, you may recall, headlining at the Flamingo. And wishing I were headlining at the Sands. To me, the Sands spelled Las Vegas success. Sinatra played there, Lena Horne, Sammy Davis, Nat King Cole, Danny Thomas—in the casino, they had painted pictures of all of them, and I wanted to be hanging there too.

But for years, Jack Entratter, the boss (and the guy who had run the old Copa), had been telling me, "You're not ready yet." He would come to every one of my opening nights, and I would have to listen to "No, not ready yet." It drove me crazy, he was like one of my uncles. In the end, his opinion was academic; I went through one more big gambling escapade and realized I was like a drunk, I couldn't handle my habit, so I left town, and stayed away for a year.

Financially, I was okay, because I was already appearing on *The Ed Sullivan Show*. Ed Sullivan had anointed me, which was a blessing; he had the most-watched show on television. After a few Sullivan shots, my price had doubled.

But I was leading two lives, one of them a total fantasy. And I almost got away with it. I was doing television—Sullivan, Garry Moore, Perry Como—and I was commuting from England—I was now more popular there than I was in the United States—and one day I came home from London with a gentleman's gentleman in tow.

His name was Bill Jones, a wonderful old auntie, the dresser at the Palladium Theatre. And he kept saying, "Danny Kaye promised he would take me to America, Dorothy Lamour promised she'd take me to America," and finally I said okay, *I'd* take him to America.

So I brought a valet into our Levittown-style bungalow, and my wife went crazy. Bill Jones had a thermometer he used when he filled my tub. Jeanette was chasing these two little kids, and I had a valet measuring the temperature of my bath water. "Get him out of here!" cried my wife.

I put Bill in a hotel until I went on tour again. The first place we headed for was the Dallas State Fair. It was summer, and when we got off the plane, it was 110 degrees. Bill Jones fainted on the tarmac. I finally traded him like a ball player to the Beach Boys, who swore they would take him to cooler places.

The next thing I brought back from London was a Rolls-Royce, and my wife went crazy again.

But this time, she could almost understand. You couldn't take money out of England, all the pounds I was earning were frozen, and somebody said to me, "If you buy a car and drive it here for a while, and then you send it home as a used car, you pay very little duty."

So I took my frozen funds, and bought the Rolls, and every day, accompanied by my friend Harry Morton, I drove from Rockville Centre to my office—by now I was juggling enough balls, writing, performing, producing, that I was renting an office—in New York. Harry, who lived in Oceanside (which wasn't far from my house), was a car freak, in addition to being an agent, a manager, and a great practical joker and con man. Besides handling acts, if you needed underwear, socks, nylons, he had them in the back of the car.

During our morning commute, he would tell me stories. One of them has become a classic. It had to do with a neighbor who came to Harry for advice about buying a new car.

Harry didn't have any patience for the long discussions enjoyed by his neighbor. "Buy the Volkswagen," he advised. "Mileage is good, it's the car of the hour."

The neighbor bought a Volkswagen but kept haranguing Harry. "He's driving me nuts," Harry said. "He holds me responsible. But I'm going to fix him."

Harry then phoned his son Robbie, who was working part-time at a gas station. "When you come home, bring me a big container of gas."

The kid brought home the gas, and that night, Harry waited for his neighbor's lights to go out. Then he went over and filled the Volkswagen's tank. Next night, another can of gas, and another refill.

Now the neighbor came to Harry. "I know you're not gonna believe this, but I'm getting a hundred fifty miles to the gallon."

"Leave me alone," said Harry, "who ever heard of a car that gets a hundred fifty miles to the gallon?"

Every night, he filled the guy's gas tank, and every morning, I got a blow-by-blow report. I finally said, "Yeah, but Harry, what's the punch line?"

It took a while to get to it. Now Harry told his son to bring him a siphon, and every night, after the neighbor went to bed, Harry siphoned off his gas, leaving just a couple of drops. The next time the guy got in the car, he drove a block, and the car stopped. He came back to Harry. "You know I told you I was getting a hundred fifty miles to the gallon? Well, I went around the corner and the car ran out of gas."

Every morning for three days, the guy filled up his tank, and every night for three nights, Harry siphoned off the gas. The guy can't drive two blocks, so now he's a basket case. Harry has a solution. "Let's go back to the Volkswagen dealer on Sunrise Highway."

Before they go, Harry calls me on the phone—remember, I've been listening to this story for weeks—and says, "Alan, you gotta be there." So I journey with him and this guy to the Volkswagen dealer.

We walk in, and Harry's neighbor collars a salesman. "I bought this car here, and for the first two, three weeks, I was getting a hundred, a hundred fifty miles to the gallon." Harry's standing behind him, making circles around his ear with his index finger, and raising his eyebrows to indicate that the salesman ought to humor this poor loony.

"Now," says the unhappy customer, "I can't go around the corner on a tank of gas."

The salesman nods sympathetically. "Why don't you leave the car here and we'll check it out."

They check it out, give it back, and the joke is over. Harry managed to convince the neighbor he'd got a car with a special experimental engine, and once the dealer realized the mistake, he'd replaced it with a regular engine.

About a year later, I went on *The Tonight Show* and told the story, and Harry's neighbor happened to be watching. He got up from his chair, walked from his house to Harry's house, rang the bell, and when Harry came to the door, the neighbor punched him right in the nose.

Harry's retired now and lives in Florida, but he was a legendary figure around Broadway.

By this time, people were beginning to ask what I felt about my success (which indicated to me that I'd moved up a notch or two in the public consciousness), and I wasn't sure what to answer. It's nice to be able to get a reservation in the best restaurants, to be able to get a seat on an airplane when nobody else can—like Mel Brooks says, "It's good to be the king"—but a lot of the pleasure for me came from the fact that my mother and father lived to see me make good.

I always talked about them in my act. And the biggest kick I got was when an Irishman or an Italian would come up afterward and say, "That was my father and my mother—so much yelling, so much love." I think maybe it had to do with the old country, the poverty of the immigrants. If *my* kids have a problem, I say, How much will it cost? But our parents had to find other ways to take care of us; they were remarkable people.

Whenever my parents came to see me perform, I'd introduce them. I'd say to the audience, "You know, I told you stories about Minnie and Bernie? Well, there is a Minnie and there is a Bernie, and there they are." My mother would slink down in her chair, my father would get up and take a bow, waving his unlit cigar in the air.

85

My mother used to say, "I never tell anybody I'm Alan King's mother." My father used to say, "I tell *everybody!*"

With me, Minnie wasn't so reticent. She would corner me: "Promise you won't get mad if I ask you something?"

If there's anything that got me mad it was when my mother would start off a conversation with "Promise me you won't get mad."

"Ma," I'd say, "I'm not going to get mad. What is it you want to ask me?"

"Well, they say—"

"Who is 'they'?"

"They say—"

"Yeah, what do they say?"

"They say you're a millionaire."

"Well, Ma, they're right."

My mother would smile serenely. "Who deserves it more than you?"

The word *millionaire* had such a ring for her, though she wasn't easy to impress. She took one look at the Rolls-Royce and said, "It's an old car." Later, when we sold the house in Rockville Centre and moved to Kings Point, my mother came from Florida to check out the new place, a half-timbered mansion built in 1926, with leaded glass windows, three stories, eight bedrooms, two dining rooms, and an elevator. And having checked it out, she said, "It's an old house."

It wasn't until after I began doing television that I finally met my father's hero, David Dubinsky. It happened because of my fondness for fashion. (I had developed a reputation for being fastidious. Jack E. Leonard once said, "Alan is so neat he steps out of the shower to take a leak.") I liked vests; I started wearing a vest on television, and the vest and the cigar became part of my persona.

Then one day I got this call that, because of me, the ILGWU was opening the first vest shop in New York in twenty-five years. (In the old days, in the twenties, a pants shop made only pants, a vest shop made only vests.)

Now the garment workers' union wanted to give me a luncheon at the Americana Hotel. And who was sitting next to me? David Dubinsky. It was late in his life, he was already retired, and he was amazed at how much I knew about the union. "Mr. Dubinsky," I said, "my father was one of your troops." Dubinsky asked my father's name, and whether he was still alive. I told him my father had retired to Florida, "That's funny," he said, "I'm going to Florida tomorrow. Write down his name and phone number."

I did it, and forgot about it. I swear, I don't think my father had ever met Dubinsky personally, though maybe he'd seen him around the union hall.

A few days later, I get a call from my father. "How's prospects?" We go through our ritual. Then he gets to the point. "You're not gonna believe who called me yesterday."

"Who?"

"Dubinsky!"

"Really?" I say. "Dubinsky called you?"

And I'm waiting for him to say that Dubinsky explained how he'd met me, but Dubinsky hadn't done that. He'd just phoned and said, "Bernie Kniberg? I'm in town, and I wanted to say hello."

I'm listening to this, and realizing it's a wonderful gift Dubinsky has made my father. So I bite on my cigar, and say, innocently, "Why would he call you?"

And my father says, "Why *shouldn't* he call me?"

Like Jerry Lewis's father *qvelling*, "Jolie remembered!"

So far, when I've talked in this book about my own idols, they've mostly been men, but throughout my career, I have met a lot of wonderful women, and for what it's worth, they make it into my pantheon too.

Besides Judy, Roz Russell, and Jane Wyman, there were also Faye Emerson, Lena Horne, and Ethel Merman—my Great Ladies.

Faye Emerson, now largely forgotten, had been a movie star and (when she was married to Elliott Roosevelt) Eleanor Roosevelt's favorite daughter-in-law. She was a fixture on early television shows, and she was gorgeous, blond, with her hair pulled back in a bun.

Faye was the first person who told me I should be an actor, not a comedian. I said, "Get off my back." But when I needed coaching as an actor, I turned to her.

The play was *Mister Roberts*. In 1955, it had opened on Broadway so successfully that regional theaters all over the country were rushing to put it on. I'd played the comedy part of Ensign Pulver a good many times, and one day I got a phone call from Bob Ludlum, the owner-manager of a theater in Fort Lee, New Jersey. (Ludlum is now a famous author.)

"I'm putting together *Mister Roberts,*" he said, "and I'd like to see you."

I wasn't interested. "I've done it too often, and besides, I'm getting too old to play Ensign Pulver."

"No," he said, "I want you to play Mr. Roberts."

I was taken aback. "Let me think about it," I said, and went off to have lunch with Nat Hiken at "21." We were sitting there when Josh Logan walked in and stopped at our table. Logan had directed the original *Mr. Roberts,* and was also coauthor of the script. He was a famously charming man, and I told him I'd had an offer to do the play in Fort Lee. "Well," he said, "you were one of the best Ensign Pulvers I ever saw."

"No," I said. "They want me to play Roberts."

He went stone-faced. "Oh," he said, and left for his own table. I was destroyed. About fifteen minutes later, he reappeared. "Why would Mr. Roberts have to come from Nebraska?" he demanded. "Why couldn't he have come from the Bronx? You do it, you play it."

He'd realized he'd wounded me, and he was a perfect gentleman, so I don't know what his real feelings were. In any case, I played the part of Roberts, and it was the best time I ever had rehearsing, because Faye Emerson coached me.

There was one little hitch. On opening night, Bob Ludlum approached me backstage. "Alan," he said, "when we get someone like you with nightclub or vaudeville ability, we like that person to come out after the final curtain and do a few minutes."

Here I'm getting paid scale for the privilege of playing Roberts, and the producer wants me to throw in my act as an encore.

I was furious. "If you think I'm going to spend two and a half hours developing this wonderful character [when Doc reads the letter from Mr. Roberts at the end, there isn't a dry eye in the place] and then, while everybody's crying, come out, take my bow, and do my act, you gotta be out of your mind."

He didn't press the point. My tutor, Faye, was proud of me.

Dr. Jekyll and Mr. Kniberg

Almost thirty years later, Faye died on the island of Ibiza. By then, they say she weighed about 350 pounds. I never knew what unhappiness sent her into exile. There was a little café called Goldie's on New York's East Side, and Goldie, who played the piano there, was another friend of Faye's. I used to stop by and ask him, "Have you heard from her?" and he'd say, "I got a Christmas card," and I'd say, "I got a Christmas card too."

Once, when I was a guest on Bill Levitt's yacht, and we anchored off Ibiza, I tried to find her. I was told that she saw no one. Learning where she lived, I went to her little house, but the maid who came to the door turned me away. The *señora* was gone. And even if she wasn't gone, the *señora* didn't entertain visitors. The *señora* said forgive me and leave me alone.

I'm still glad I knew her, if only for a little while.

Lena? For years and years, I opened her show. Then she quit working. She'd lost her father, she'd lost her son, and Lennie Hayton (to whom she'd been married for many years) had died too. After all this, Lena just retreated into herself. Her family and friends were concerned. Her daughter Gail called me. "Alan, we've got to do something about Mother."

I'd already been calling Lena from time to time to ask how she was doing, but she hadn't encouraged my inquiries. Now, I was about to go into Caesar's Palace in Las Vegas, and I went to visit her—she was living up on Lexington Avenue—and after some small talk, I told her I wanted her to be on the show with me.

"I can't work," she said.

"You're gonna work," I said. "You're too young, you're too great." We had a real fight, and I thought I'd lost.

Next day I got a call from her manager, Ralph Harris. "I don't know what you did," he said, "but Lena says she's going into Caesar's Palace with you."

And that was how she started her comeback.

She came to a Friars dinner in my honor—by that time, she'd enjoyed a triumphal return to Broadway—and with the humility I'm so famous for, I emceed the dinner myself. I said nobody could do it better. (By then, Jessel was dead.)

I was standing up there, and suddenly Lena, who wasn't scheduled

89

to speak, and who's very shy, rose and announced that she'd like to say a few words. And the audience started applauding, and she told the story about how I'd shown up at her apartment. "And he said, 'If you don't get back to work, I'll kick your ass.' "

I hope I was more delicate than that, but even if I wasn't, you have to admit my crudeness was in a good cause.

Another time, I tried to force Ethel Merman back to work, but in her case, I was less successful. I wanted her to do a musical—it was based on a Bruce Jay Friedman novel called *A Mother's Kisses*—to which I'd bought the rights. Ethel had just divorced Bob Six, who was president of Continental Airlines, and I remember sitting in her Park Avenue living room, surrounded by her art collection, while she assured me that she would never play Broadway again.

"Why not?" I asked.

She told me. "Because when I'm doing a show, I work so hard. If I do eight shows a week, I can't go out after the theater. And when I get home, there's nobody there. I'm not doing another play, I'm not coming home alone to this empty apartment."

It was pitiful. Merman, the ball breaker of the Western world, but she was lonely.

Being a strong woman and having a strong marriage don't necessarily go together. I could give you a list of strong women who had husbands that were like valets. I once asked a friend who managed his wife, "Do you ever have sex with her?" "Only," he said, "if it will further her career."

My own career—insofar as the movies were concerned—was going nowhere. I was playing the same part over and over again, either the nice guy who doesn't get the girl, or some sergeant from Brooklyn named Kowalski, so I elected to go on suspension.

I just wanted to leave California, and I got in my car and drove away.

Ten years later, when Warners' was opening *Who's Afraid of Virginia Woolf?* at the Criterion Theater in New York, Jack Warner put me to work again.

It was a big night. Elizabeth Taylor and Richard Burton would be in attendance—the profits from the premiere were to go to a charity dear to Philip Burton, Richard's foster father and acting coach—and after the movie, there was to be a party at the Astor Roof.

Harry Mayer, who booked the Strand Theater for Warners', had called me. "Jack wants to know if you'll emcee; he'd like to introduce you as toastmaster of the evening."

I said I'd love to.

Now I'm sitting on the dais, and Jack, my old boss—who never even knew I'd been under contract to him—gets up and starts telling a story. He could talk, this guy. So he explains how he went into a small nightclub in California and saw a young man and realized this was somebody special. I'm wondering, Who's he talking about?

"I discovered this boy," he says. "And had he not wanted to go on and become a great comedian, he could have become a fine actor."

Eight hundred, a thousand people were in the ballroom, and Jack winds up, "Here he is. I take great pride in introducing my protégé, Alan King."

Big round of applause.

I rose, looked around the room, and in my best Jack Benny delivery, drawled, "Jack, you're full of shit," and Richard Burton laughed so hard he fell backward off the dais.

9 ∞ MORE VEGAS NIGHTS

And Noah he often said to his wife when he sat down to dine,
I don't care where the water goes if it doesn't get into the wine.

—G. K. CHESTERTON

ALL THROUGH THAT YEAR I'd stayed away from Las Vegas, I still dreamed of appearing on the stage of the Sands Hotel. And then a guy named Stan Irwin, an old comic who was Johnny Carson's manager, became the booker at the Sahara, and he offered me a ton of money to come there.

I said I just wouldn't work Vegas, I couldn't trust myself.

But my manager, Harry Adler, solved the problem. "I'll tell you what we'll do," he said. "We'll hire a bodyguard, and he'll live with you, in the room with you, he'll be with you twenty-four hours a day."

So that's what happened. I went back to Vegas.

My bodyguard—he wasn't really my bodyguard, he was my keeper—was Mickey Shaw, an ex-fighter, a kind of character around Broadway who had been one of the special police at Yankee Stadium.

But even without him, I would probably have behaved. I'd been away a year, and I had a lot to prove; if I couldn't play Vegas, my pride told me I might as well get out of the business.

Opening night, Jack ("You're not ready") Entratter came to the show, and afterward, he appeared in my dressing room. "You're ready," he said.

So I got to play the Sands. For eighteen years. I remember the first time I went into the casino, and there was an oil painting of me—they just had somebody copy it off a publicity shot, a black-and-white glossy—and it was hanging on the wall with Sammy and Frank. To me, it was like getting an Academy Award.

Entratter was one tough son of a bitch, a big guy with hands like hams, and a big heart, too. He used to sit in the back booth every night. I'd quit gambling, but I hadn't given up drinking, so by the second show, I was generally half loaded, and I wouldn't get off the stage. It would drive Entratter crazy.

He would come back and warn me. "We got a casino out there, and you're the shill to get 'em into the casino. If you do more than your allotted time, I'm turnin' off the lights."

I'd be doing the second show, feeling no pain, the audience having a great time, and I'd see the lights begin to blink. And I'd say, "Ladies and gentlemen, there is nothing wrong with the electricity, it's just that the man who owns this place wants me to get off the stage. Do *you* want me to get off the stage?" They'd yell, "Nooo," and Entratter would get so mad, he'd pull a switch, and we'd have a blackout.

"Ladies and gentlemen," I'd say, "everybody take out a match and light it, I'm not leaving."

This continued until one night I was carrying on, and out of the audience came two sheriffs, each about eight feet tall and wearing sidearms. They started for me, one from each side of the stage. Entratter's yelling, "Go get him, drag him off," and I'm screaming, "Ladies and gentlemen, you are now witnessing something that should be reported in every newspaper. My civil rights are being abused."

It was a riot; whenever my act ran too long, they used to drag me off the stage.

While I was working for Entratter, I started a precedent. I said I wanted to do a performance at 2:30 in the morning, because everyone in town was doing two shows a night, eight o'clock and midnight, and we could never see each other work. Jack liked the idea, so once during every engagement, we invited all the acts from other shows. Soon a lot of places were doing the same thing.

Those years were the heart of my career, and Vegas was like one long New Year's Eve. I don't enjoy the town now, it's Disneyland with crap tables. When I'm drinking, I don't want to see two pirate ships sinking in front of me.

The new Las Vegas is for kiddies, but back in the fifties and sixties, it was a gambling town for grown-ups, for high rollers and swingers. Benny Siegel said, "Las Vegas turns women into men, and men into idiots." What a place. Great fortunes were made there in real estate, too. Somebody would say, "I'm buying that corner for eleven dollars," and you'd laugh, but a lot of actors were smart enough to snap up property. I wasn't one of them.

I loved to write Las Vegas jokes. "When the plane comes in, the stewardess says, 'We're about to land, fasten your money belt,' " and "When you see Las Vegas from the air it looks like a vacuum cleaner," and my all-time favorite, "A guy rode into town in a ten-thousand-dollar Cadillac, and went home in a hundred-thousand-dollar bus."

I lived through all the changes in Las Vegas, from the mob guys to Howard Hughes. Hughes came there and started buying up the town. He bought the Desert Inn, the Flamingo, the Landmark—half the property on the Strip—and finally, the jewel in Vegas's crown, the Sands.

When Jack Entratter sold out to Hughes, I figured my obligation to the Sands was over. Everybody had worked for Jack for less money than they could have got elsewhere because we were a family. I'm not complaining—I was getting $25,000 a week—but I'd been turning down offers of a lot more from other places.

The family was disintegrating anyway. Sinatra had a big fight with one of the Sands' bosses, a guy by the name of Carl Cohen, and Frank just picked up and moved over to Caesar's Palace. I got a call in New York in the middle of the night. "Sinatra walked," Carl Cohen said. "You gotta get out here and replace him right away."

When I arrived, the Sands was like a war zone, and Howard Hughes had become the invisible man. Still, he knew everything that was going on. Everyone believed all the important rooms in the Sands were bugged, and that Hughes was listening in on everybody.

I'd walk into an empty dressing room and shout, "How are ya, Howard? Alan here." Wherever I went, I'd talk to Howard. I'd go up to a lamp: "Howard, how you feeling?"

It was a joke that paid off. One night Charlie Turner—a holdover from the Entratter regime who had stayed on at the Sands—came backstage to talk to me. "Alan, I hear you're not happy here."

"Charlie," I said, "I'm not."

"Okay," he said, "what will make you happy?"

"Money," I said. And I started screaming at the ceiling. "You hear me, Howard? Money!"

Next day, a couple of Howard's representatives showed up with a new offer. "We'll double your salary, we'll give you fifty thousand a week, nine weeks a year, three three-week engagements."

The Sands still felt like home, so I said okay. Next day, a well-dressed man—everybody who worked for Hughes looked like an FBI agent—came and handed me a little box. Inside was a pair of cufflinks, exact duplicates of the drill bit Howard's father had invented, the bit on which the Hughes fortune was built.

It was a badge of honor. After the man left, I sat down at my dressing table, looked into the mirror, and said, "Thank you, Howard!"

I finished out the year.

By now, the mob guys were fading—having worked the Sands through the sixties and into the early seventies, I'd seen it happen—and a bidding war for my services was going on. I was playing off the Riviera against Caesar's Palace; each had offered $75,000 a week, and then $100,000 a week, enormous, unprecedented money for me.

Now came the moment of truth. Caesar's Palace had just changed hands, bought by a man named Cliff Perlman, who'd made a fortune with a fast-food business in Florida. I met in an office with two of his representatives. They were Billy Weinberger, one of the bosses and hosts of Caesar's Palace, and Sid Gathrid, its entertainment director.

"We'll give you twelve weeks a year, at one hundred thousand a week," Billy said.

I sat there. One of my many problems was that I used to conduct most of my own business, and I was trying not to grin.

"What can we do to sweeten the pot?" asked Sid.

I thought a minute. "I want my own tennis tournament."

They laughed.

I persisted. "I want a professional tennis tournament."

They were typical gamblers; they looked at each other, looked at me, and one of them said, "You're faded."

That's how the Alan King Tennis Classic at Caesar's Palace was born. It became the single biggest attraction in town, the Siegfried and Roy of its day. And because money seemed to have no meaning whatsoever in Las Vegas, we started with a $50,000 prize, then moved it up to $100,000, and were condemned by *Tennis* magazine: "Alan King and his Las Vegas mentality will ruin the game." (In the late eighties, after seventeen years in Las Vegas, we moved the tournament to Palm Springs, where we built the Grand Champion Hotel. In 1995, the prize money was $1,750,000.)

At Caesar's Palace, I had carte blanche. I started bringing in major acts to share the bill with me. I had Ella Fitzgerald, I had Lena Horne twice, I had Peggy Lee twice, and Anthony Newley and Carol Channing. They'd do the first half of the show, I'd do the second half, then at the end we'd come out and do an afterpiece together.

I had incredible good times, but unlike a lot of acts that played Vegas sixteen, twenty weeks a year, and settled down there, I never thought of living anywhere but New York. Still, in some ways, I spent a lifetime in Las Vegas, and I often think about some of the people I spent it with.

When I first went to work for Ben Siegel, I met a guy named Georgie Capri. (It wasn't his real name, but he came from Capri.) He looked like Sky Masterson, in his dark shirt and white tie. He was handsome, nice, a great ladies' man, and he was a host at the Flamingo.

Like George Raft, another nice guy who served as a host in Las Vegas—Raft had got into a mess over income taxes, and watched his movie career disappear—Georgie Capri had been in trouble with the law, which seemed to have left him with a soft spot for any other loser.

In my gambling days, when I'd be tapped out, Georgie was always good for a loan. He had a cash box in a cage at the Flamingo, and I'd go to him—"Georgie, I need money"—and he'd give it to me. "Okay, you got five thousand, no more."

One day he and I were schmoozing, and he said he'd never been back to visit his native island. "My family left Italy when I was a child."

I was flabbergasted. "You've been in jail, you were on the isle of Alcatraz, and you've never been back to the isle of Capri? You gotta go to Capri." (Jeanette and I had been there, and we loved it.)

But Georgie had other things on his mind; he was in the middle of a big romance with Peggy Lee. The next time I heard from him, he and Peggy had split up, and I was back in New York. He called from Las Vegas. "I'm coming East, we'll have dinner, and where do you think I'm going then? I'm going to Capri!"

In those days, you couldn't fly nonstop from Las Vegas to New York; you had to go to Denver or Chicago and change planes. So Georgie goes to Chicago, picks up a Chicago paper, and reads that Peggy Lee is playing the Palmer House. He phones her—after all, they're still friends—and she says, "Ah, Georgie, why don't you come to the hotel, we'll have dinner, you'll see the show, and you can take a plane to New York tomorrow."

So I get another call from Georgie. "Our date is off, Peggy's in town, I'm going to stay over."

The next day, I'm listening to the radio and it says a United Airlines plane and a TWA plane crashed over Staten Island in the harbor. Everyone was killed. Georgie was on one of those planes, and Peggy Lee never forgot it. She's felt guilty about it for thirty years.

10 ∾ Other Voices

HAVING DISCOVERED the joys of London with Judy Garland, I spent as much time as I could there, and I not only appeared before the Queen of England, I also got to know the king of the British theater, Laurence Olivier. He was a brilliant, modest, sad man.

We met at the Dominion Theatre when Judy and I were appearing there. He came backstage and wanted to talk craft, he was always fascinated by the work. (He himself played—brilliantly—a burnt-out song-and-dance man in John Osborne's *The Entertainer*.)

In his later years, he suffered from cancer, which didn't prevent his playing *Othello* (on stage, at that, eight times a week), though it's one of the most difficult roles an actor can attempt. And it was especially difficult for him, because he had a naturally high voice. In order to bring it down, he practiced the Moor's deep resonance every waking moment.

I was set to do a television show in London, and I'd written to say I was on my way across the Atlantic and would like to see him. "You must come to the theatre," he wrote back. "We'll have supper afterward."

His Othello was not only arduous but the subject of much debate. He played the Moor in blackface, with red lips, and some people objected, saying that it was as though he were doing a minstrel show. But I was awed.

After the final curtain, Jeanette and I went backstage where his wife, Joan Plowright, was standing guard. She asked us to give him some time. "He's so exhausted." We knew he was sick—everybody knew he was sick—and I felt so bad. "No, no," I said, "just tell him we thought he was wonderful." "No, no," she said right back, "he wants to see you, but he needs to rest for a few minutes."

There was a pub across the street, and we went over and ordered beer. A couple of guys who recognized me from English television began kibitzing, and after a half hour or so, we went back to the theater. Again Joan Plowright intercepted us. Would Mrs. King mind waiting? "Larry would like to see Alan."

I walked into the dressing room, and he was sitting in his robe in front of the mirror with the white lights around it. He still hadn't taken off his makeup, the black was all streaked, and he was leaning on the dressing table, looking at his reflection, and he said, "Alan, what's a grown man doing, putting on this crazy face? It's *kinderspiel.*"

Kinderspiel. Child's play. I'll never forget it as long as I live, he said it with such despair.

He was a worrier, whether he was playing tragedy or comedy. He thought comedy was the most difficult art in the world. Once he saw me at a Variety Club benefit, and came backstage. "How do you do it, dear boy? How do you do it?"

In 1967, at the National Theatre, he appeared in a minor role in Molière's *A Flea in Her Ear*—he was the butler—and when I visited him afterward, he said, "Did you notice how I worked with the tie?" And he flicked his necktie the way Stan Laurel used to do. In order to play comedy, he had to remember having seen someone else do something funny.

He always said he was an external actor, that he needed to put a nose on, and think how the character looked physically before he could find him. Once I asked him, "Who's the greatest actor you ever saw?" I thought he would say Richardson or Gielgud. He said Marlon Brando.

I was thrilled, because I'd always believed that Marlon Brando was the greatest actor *I* ever saw.

Once I spent a weekend in a house where Brando was also a guest. It was in Runnymede, near Windsor Castle; Elliott Kastner and Tessa Kennedy, mutual friends, were our hosts. Marlon, who then weighed over 300 pounds, had just traveled alone all over Europe. He wore a Greek sailor's hat, and he said nobody recognized him. He also said he couldn't fly on the Concorde because he couldn't fit in the seat.

I asked him the same question I'd asked Olivier. "Who's the greatest actor you ever saw?" He didn't miss a beat. "Paul Muni," he said.

Muni, my first hero. Probably because my parents had taken me to the Yiddish theater to see him when his name was still Muni Weisenfreund. I got to know him toward the end of his life, when he was doing *Inherit the Wind* on Broadway, which seemed only right because he was playing another of my heroes, Clarence Darrow. (How could I, child of an old socialist, not pay tribute to Darrow?)

I talked to Marlon about Muni and the Yiddish theater, and it turned out Marlon could speak Yiddish. I was taken aback. "Where did you learn?"

"You told me you knew everything about me," he said. "But you didn't know I was practically raised by the Adler family. My teacher was Stella Adler, Jacob Adler's daughter, and the Adlers were gods of the Yiddish theater. And I'll tell you something else. That Ben Hecht play, *A Flag Is Born*, about the birth of the state of Israel? I played a spear-carrier; Paul Muni was the star, and most of my time offstage I spent in the wings watching him."

The last years of Muni's life were very sad. He was losing his eyesight, he was losing his hearing, and when they did the television version of *Inherit the Wind* at a studio in Brooklyn, I went there to watch him. He wore an earpiece, they were feeding him his lines through it, but if you see it on kinescope, you can't tell.

A long time afterward, when I was making *Memories of Me,* I carried a picture of Muni as a sort of talisman. Billy Crystal had written the movie, and it just broke my heart, it was so sad.

I was playing this very unsuccessful extra, and in one scene, I had a big fight with Billy, who was playing my son. He said, "You're not an actor, you're an extra!" and I said, "No, I'm *king* of the extras!"

My character was a total failure who lived in a dream world, and when I was thinking about it, I decided I needed an image to inspire me. Extras always carry a little suitcase with them; they've got everything in it. You see them with the folding chair in the morning when they're sitting around waiting to be called; they have the coffee thermos in the suitcase, and a deck of cards, and the trade papers, and maybe some cigarettes.

All through that movie, I carried a little suitcase, with a picture of Paul Muni taped inside the lid. *Memories of Me* was my *Lear.* I'll never get a chance to do anything like it again.

I was producing the picture as well as acting in it, and Billy and I agreed that we needed something to show that the old man was losing his mind, and I suggested a speech from *Inherit the Wind.* Because at the end of that play, after the reporter says to Darrow, "You did it! William Jennings Bryan was an idiot," something like that, Darrow turns on him. "No, no, no," he says. "Do you know what it's like to walk down an empty street, with the shutters closed?" He understood, he felt for the Bryan character.

So now we're shooting the last scene of *Memories of Me,* where I'm dead, and the box is about to be lowered into the ground, and Billy is going to do the eulogy. We were using the Cemetery of the Stars, but Billy didn't want me to be anywhere near the place. "If you're on location, I'm not going to be able to do the eulogy."

I said okay. Then I went away and hired a guy with a pickup truck and I lay down in the back of the truck, covered myself with blankets, and while they were shooting the scene, I—the banished but resourceful producer—rode around peering out from under the blankets.

After several hours, I hear someone say, "It's a wrap!" and I see them starting to pack up the equipment, so I appear. And Billy says,

"Everybody knew you were in the back of that truck, everybody! Everybody!"

The crew is laughing, and Billy says, "Now I'm gonna tell you a crazy story. Here's a map of this cemetery. Right across from where we've been shooting, Paul Muni is buried."

I thought it was a gag until I looked at the map. While the crew finished breaking down the set, I went off to search for Muni's grave in section 8 H. But there were hundreds of graves. I must have spent an hour hunting, and I was going crazy. Finally, I presented myself and the map at the cemetery office. "It says Paul Muni is buried here, and I can't find him."

They got a workman to help me, and we uncovered the grave. Literally uncovered. It was under six feet of weeds and grass, and nobody to take care of it, nobody. He had no family there. He lay alone under a black stone, and all the stone said was MUNI.

I went back to my crew, who were still in 8 H. "Guys, I need a favor." The grips came with me, and we cleaned up the site. I'd met the man only a few times, but I felt I owed him.

Muni not only distinguished himself onstage, he had a thirty-year career in films (four Academy Award nominations, one win, for *The Story of Louis Pasteur*). But he was never an American icon like John Wayne.

Wayne was a different kind of movie star than Muni. Muni was always a character actor, Duke was always Duke. His strength lay in bending a role to his own personality, rather than submerging his personality in a role. "I play John Wayne in every picture, regardless of the character," he said, "and I've been doing all right, haven't I?"

The first time I ever mentioned John Wayne—in public, that is—was on a Dick Cavett show back during the Vietnam War. Mary Travers, of Peter, Paul and Mary, was also a guest, and so was a member of the Nixon White House staff, Herb Klein. We were having this big debate about the war. Mary was very upset, but I was trying to speak calmly. I thought we were losing our point by being so emotional; we were making the supporters of the war sound like the rational ones.

Anyway, I suggested that the people in this country had a John Wayne mentality. I'd never met John Wayne, and I didn't say anything bad about John Wayne, but I was against what I believed John Wayne represented. "My country right or wrong," I said. "I heard that in Nuremberg."

Fade to Acapulco the following winter. I'd finished playing tennis, and I was with a bunch of guys sitting and drinking around a big piano bar that was carved out of stone. My wife was upstairs getting dressed for dinner, but in Acapulco, nobody went to dinner before ten o'clock, so I always had a nice long cocktail hour. All of a sudden, I felt a hand on my shoulder.

I looked around, and it was a hand as big as a foot. I never saw a hand so big. It had size, it had weight, and its owner loomed over me, appearing to be ten feet tall.

"I hear," he said, "that you've had things to say about me." I stood up, as he continued. "But I also hear we've got a lot of mutual friends, so why don't we have a drink and talk about it?"

He was a giant. I've known taller men, and I've known wider men, but I've never known anybody else that looked like John Wayne.

So we start talking about this one and that one, and I'm tap-dancing pretty good, I'm gonna be Charlie Charming, I don't want John Wayne mad at me. He's reminiscing about Toots Shor, I'm telling stories, we're discussing sportswriters, and we're drinking and drinking and drinking, and I'm having the best time. He's a great audience, and he's laughing. Now we're at a round bar, away from the piano bar, and the phone rings.

It's my wife. "What are you, crazy?" she inquires. "Where the hell are you? It's quarter to ten, I'm all dressed, and we're supposed to be going to dinner with people—"

I interrupt her. "Jeanette," I say, "I'm getting drunk with John Wayne."

"Right," she says, "and I am having sex with Paul Newman." And she hangs up the phone.

I'm laughing, and Big John wants to know why, so I tell him.

"Oh yeah?" says Wayne. "Well, we'll just take care of that." And he walks me to our penthouse. You had to climb up maybe four flights of stairs that curled around the side of a mountain, and when we got there, Jeanette was stunned—but still funny. She took a breath, then turned and shouted toward the bedroom, "Paul, come out and say hello to John Wayne."

Even people whose politics were very different from his ended up loving John Wayne. Katharine Hepburn, a great liberal, enjoyed making *Rooster Cogburn* with him, and Lauren Bacall, who'd vowed she'd never work with him, played his landlady in *The Shootist*, and found the experience good. Everybody knew he was an archconservative, but he was also the most gentlemanly, the nicest, man. (In *The Shootist*, he was cast as an old ex-gunfighter dying of cancer. He himself was dying of cancer at the time.)

Wayne made more movies than any other major star—his first in 1927, his last in 1976—but was unpretentious about himself and his career. "I never had a goddamn artistic problem in my life, never," he said once, "and I've worked with the best of them. John Ford isn't exactly a bum, is he? Yet he never gave me any manure about art."

After Wayne died, a public school was built in Williamsburg, Brooklyn, and the kids of the neighborhood, by then entirely Hispanic and black, were invited to name it. They voted to call it the John Wayne School. They could have honored Lupe Velez, or Juarez, or Malcolm X, but they chose John Wayne.

All of Wayne's children were coming East for the dedication, and since I'd grown up in Williamsburg, one of John's sons asked if I would come too.

So I was there, and in the course of the ceremonies, I talked to these kids who were inhabitants of the streets where Alex Jabofsky and I had once run wild. And I told them about John Wayne and me. I said here were two men at opposite ends of the political spectrum, and yet we became friends. I was trying to make the kids understand that such a thing was possible.

I liked John Wayne. I still wear a western hat he sent me.

Over the years, I've lost a lot of my heroes, but the death that tore me up the most was probably Jack Benny's.

Jack and I went back a long way, all the way back to Leon and Eddie's, in fact. When Jack, Bob Hope, George Burns were in New York, they used to come in to Leon and Eddie's on Sunday nights, and there I was doing "Bumps-a-Daisy." Whether or not they were impressed with my youthful bravado, I can't say.

By the time I started working on the Sullivan shows, I'd almost forgotten I'd met Jack, and I certainly wasn't counting on his remembering me. Then one night my phone rang at home, and this voice said, "It's Jack Benny."

The Sullivan show was broadcast live in the East, but it used to be delayed for California, where it was heard three hours later. So I was already home in Rockville Centre on this Sunday night when the call came. I thought it was somebody kidding me, maybe Larry Storch doing a Jack Benny. Again the caller spoke. "Alan, this is Jack."

"Yeah," I said. "Sure."

"For God's sake," he said, "what do I have to do, play 'Love in Bloom'? This is Jack Benny, I just saw you on the Sullivan show, and you were wonderful."

He had gone to a lot of trouble—he'd phoned around, and finally reached my agent, Lou Weiss, who was also George Burns's nephew— to find my number, but that's what he was like, that's what Jack Benny was about. After that, every time I finished a Sullivan show, I got a call from Jack.

Whenever I was in Los Angeles, I'd phone him, and he'd say, "Come on, have lunch."

Which meant the Hillcrest Country Club. Jack, George Burns, Georgie Jessel, Groucho Marx, Danny Kaye, Abe Lastfogel (Abe wasn't a comic, he was head of the William Morris Agency), Lou Holtz would be sitting at the same big round table. I'd walk in, and Jessel would stand up and announce me. "That's Alan King, and anybody don't like him can kiss my ass!" That was my intro.

(The first time Jessel watched me work, he indicated a kind of wonder. "You're the best I've seen since Sam Bernard," he said. I was delighted, but no matter how many people in the business I pumped, I couldn't find out anything about this Sam Bernard. Finally, I went to Joe E. Lewis. "Who's Sam Bernard?" "Oh," said Joe E., "you've been talking to Jessel. There is no Sam Bernard, he tells that to everybody.")

Jessel would often wear an army uniform covered with medals; he was outrageous but hilarious, special. And as a toastmaster, nobody came close to him. President Roosevelt had proclaimed him Toastmaster General of the United States.

At Hillcrest, I just sat and listened to the big boys. They were funny, and they knew they were funny; it was fireworks, each of them trying to outdo the others. Groucho never stopped (if you tell forty jokes, three of them are bound to work) but even Groucho shut up when Jessel was holding forth. Jack was the only relatively quiet one; offstage, he was an introverted man.

Late in his life, he had an opening at Caesar's Palace, and a big junket of Hollywood people flew in to Vegas to see him. I think I was opening the next night at the Sands, I don't remember. I know I didn't come on the junket, and yet I was there.

Jack did two shows that night. The place was loaded with stars, and he came out and got a standing ovation, an ovation befitting a legend.

He went through the first show. He had this little girl who played the violin, he had the orangutans he worked with, the audience was whistling, applauding, and then it was over.

Backstage, there were so many celebrities you couldn't breathe; all of Hollywood was in the greenroom, which was a big chamber with an open bar. Off this was a small dressing room with a shower, the place where Jack changed and did his makeup. He was standing in his robe, and across the crowd—in a room that should have held twenty-five and had a hundred—he was waving at me, signaling me to come over.

I fought my way through his other admirers, and he took me by the arm, led me into the little dressing room, and shut the door.

"Jack, you were fabulous," I began, but he stopped me. "Cut the bullshit," he said. "What went wrong?"

"Come on," I said. "Are you kidding? You heard the laughs, you heard the applause—"

"Don't jerk me around," he said. "Just tell me what went wrong."

Jack Benny asking Alan King for advice? I took a deep breath. "Jack, you were doing an impression of yourself out there. It was Rich Little doing Jack Benny. The 'well' took a little longer, the gestures, when you put your hand to your face, took a little longer—"

He nodded, cutting me off. "Come back and see the second show." I stood for the second show, and he was bang, bang, bang, right on the nose. My God, that fraction of a second that he speeded things up made all the difference. When I went backstage, another crowd was waiting to kiss him, and he was standing across the greenroom again in the same spot where I'd seen him earlier. I just gave him the thumbs-up sign and went out into the street.

Once he and I were paired as presenters at the Tony Awards, though generally, a man is teamed up with a woman. Jack complained. "How come everybody else got a beautiful girl, and I got you?" I said, "Jack, if you play your cards right—" and he said, "Oh, cut that out," the way only Jack could say it.

He and George Burns were like Damon and Pythias, closer than lovers, closer than brothers. Many years ago, when George had his quadruple bypass, I went with Jack to visit him. He was just out of the hospital, wearing a beret so he didn't have to bother with his toupee, and he held his cigar, but it wasn't lit.

Everybody thought George would go first, and that Jack would live forever—after all, he was eternally thirty-nine—but it was the other way around. Jack died before he could play in the movie version of *The Sunshine Boys*, and George got the part.

A lot of famous actors had wanted to play *The Sunshine Boys*, those two crotchety old vaudevillians. Phil Silvers had tested, so had Red Skelton. In fact, Jack did a test with Red. Early in the morning, in the makeup room, Herb Ross, the director, gave Jack instructions: "Now in this scene, you get into an argument with Red, he'll go into the kitchen, and you'll go right after him to continue the argument."

The rehearsal begins. Skelton walks to the kitchen door, and Jack is right on top of him. "Cut," says Herb, and takes Jack aside. "You gotta understand, you're using too much energy, slow down, your character is supposed to be in his late seventies."

"Well," says Jack, "I'm *eighty*."

They do it again, same thing. Red walks too slow, Jack walks too fast, he keeps climbing up Red's back, and whenever Herb Ross says, "The man is in his late seventies," Jack says—again—"But I'm *eighty*."

I was driving when I heard over the car radio that Jack had been taken ill—he'd been playing Dallas—and was in the hospital. I stopped at a phone booth, called the hospital, and they said he was doing fine.

Later I heard another bulletin. He was dead.

I called George. George, who was closer to Jack than anybody, even his children, George, who had been his friend for more than sixty years. When he answered the phone, I said, "George, it's Alan, I just had to call you." And he said, simply, "It's going to be very lonely," and I started to cry.

11 ∾ FRANK

All those little girls, they followed Frank.

HERE'S A strongly held opinion: Frank Sinatra is far and away the greatest singer of popular music our society has known. In a hundred years, they'll be teaching Einstein's theory to mathematicians and scientists, and in a hundred years, when people get together to study pop music, Sinatra will be taught—for his phrasing, his musicianship, his style; when it comes to swinging, he kicks ass.

That out of the way, let me say it: I hate Frank Sinatra. My wife has been in love with him for fifty-five years. I remember standing in the park one Saturday night in Williamsburg, waiting for Jeanette—in her bobby socks—to come home from the Paramount, where she'd sat through six shows. To this day, whenever she's around Frank, she melts. And he knows it, and plays it for all it's worth. Just recently, after a dinner with him in Palm Springs, we came back to the hotel and she was still carrying on. "Isn't he great? Isn't he wonderful?"

"He's fuckin' old," I said. "It's enough already with Frank."

But if anybody has a right to be old, it's Frank, because he's lived so many lives. Good, bad, and indifferent.

No. Forget indifferent. He's never indifferent.

He has a tough-guy mentality, and he lives by an ancient code; he's unforgiving of his enemies, protective of his friends. After Spiro Agnew became a pariah, totally discredited, he was living in Palm Springs at Frank's house. People would ask why, and Frank would say, "He's my friend."

If you're his friend, you're his friend forever, no moral judgments involved. In the old days, the Chicago mob boys, Joe Fischetti, Sam Giancana, hung around him, and he made no apologies for that. "When I was down, when I was broke, when I lost my voice, these were the only guys that helped me," he said. "What do you want me to do now?"

Once I came to meet him in a restaurant, and he was sitting at a table with a group—I didn't know any of them—and he seemed distraught. There was a big grand jury investigation going on in New Jersey, and he was complaining that the press kept picking on him because of his "so-called affiliation" with mob guys. "Why don't they talk about my relationships with presidents? With people of culture? Why do they always talk about my mob associations?"

And then he said, "Oh, by the way, Alan, say hello to the guys, this is Willie the Nose, Hymie the Hook, Nick the Knife—" I started to laugh, and he bristled. "What are you laughing at?"

"Nothing, Frank," I said. "Nothing."

We first met in Atlantic City. I was booked to open for him on a Memorial Day, at the Steel Pier, and I was very excited. I'd followed his career from the early Harry James days through his first big recording of "All or Nothing at All," and his switch to Tommy Dorsey's band. I admired him greatly, though I wouldn't say so because of all those teenyboppers jumping up and down and yelling, "Frankie! Frankie!"

Sinatra had just left Dorsey; he was now a single, and he had agreed to play the Steel Pier for one week, six shows a day.

The night before we opened, I was still in Pike, New Hampshire, working the Lake Tarleton Club. I finished my final set there, got into my old De Soto, and drove south. There were no superhighways then, I just hung my head out of the window and drove, arriving in Atlantic City in time—barely—to make the 10 A.M. show. On my way to the dressing rooms, I noticed that Frank's door was guarded, and outside of it there stood a big old-fashioned red cooler loaded with Coca-Cola. In those days, he was a big Coke drinker. Since I hadn't slept, I took a cold shower, got dressed, went onstage—I still hadn't seen Frank—and got a lot of laughs. I was supposed to do twelve minutes, but I did eighteen. When I walked off, there was Frank standing in the wings. I said, "Hello, Mr. Sinatra." He said, "Next time, try twelve."

In that one week, Sunday to Saturday, we did forty-two shows, and before the last one, the owner of the Pier, George Hamid (accompanied by the fire chief), came back to talk to us. "People are lined up on the boardwalk for a mile, there are so many of them we're afraid the boardwalk could collapse."

Frank thought for a couple of seconds. At the end of the pier, there was an enormous pavilion where name bands played for dancing. "Let's move the show to the ballroom," he said. "And let 'em all in, even the ones without tickets."

"What are you, crazy?" said George.

"You got two choices," said Frank. "You got chaos, or you let 'em in."

George saw the wisdom in Frank's argument, but he was still grumbling, "How'm I gonna collect the money from these people?" as he left.

There were police and firemen standing by—it was total pandemonium—and they let everybody into the ballroom. The people stood packed together like sardines. I came on, did two jokes, said, "Here he is, Frank Sinatra," and got out of his way.

Though he and I became friends, I was never one of Frank's inner circle, never a member of the Rat Pack. As a young married man, I had other priorities. This sometimes irritated Frank, because he doesn't extend invitations, he just tells you, "We're going." I remember there was a heavyweight fight in Stockholm, and he was flying over there with some pals, and he wanted me to come along. I said, "Frank, I can't, I gotta open in London the next day," and he got pissed off.

About a week later, I picked up the London papers, and there was a picture of Sinatra and Co. at the fight. The caption under the picture read: "Frank and his Mafia bodyguards." I got hysterical. There were Martin Gabel (four foot eight, with bad feet and chronic arthritis); Harry Muffson, the owner of the Eden Roc Hotel in Miami (recovering from his third angina attack); Prince Mike Romanoff (who was even smaller and sicker than Martin Gabel); and the venerable Joe E. Lewis, who'd just had half his stomach removed. Frank, surrounded by old men. Look at this Mafia, this protection he had.

Frank shared my affection for Swifty Morgan, the hustler who walked the streets of Miami with jewelry wrapped in tissue paper stashed in every pocket. When he'd hand you some cockamamie trinket, he'd always say, "Take it, you'll see me later," and we'd buy cufflinks, stickpins, whatever he had.

One day Swifty and I were having a sandwich, and when it came time to pay his bill, he took out a gold money clip on which was a replica, in relief, of the Torah, the sacred text that contains the five books of Moses. It was beautiful, I wanted it. The idea that God and Mammon were not natural allies didn't occur to me at the time.

"Swifty," I said, "instead of showing me all that junk jewelry, sell me the money clip."

"It's not for sale," said Swifty.

"Swifty," I said, "everything you got is for sale, including your teeth."

"Don't be such a smart guy," he said. "My good friend, the late, great Rabbi Wise, on his deathbed, gave me this treasure."

I became obsessed with the money clip. Every day for a week, I badgered Swifty. "I gotta have it."

Finally he capitulated. "You're driving me nuts, give me five hundred." I said I didn't have five hundred. "Okay," he said, "you'll pay me when you got it."

It was one of my proudest possessions. About a year later, I was having dinner with Sinatra in La Rue, a Beverly Hills restaurant, and he whipped out a gold money clip with a Torah on it. I couldn't believe it. "Where did you get that?"

"Oh," he said, "it's a great story. On his deathbed, Rabbi Wise gave it to Swifty Morgan."

I produced my copy of the money clip. "The rabbi," I said, "must have been awfully busy on his deathbed handing out these damn things."

If Swifty hustled Frank and me, we tortured him too. Once, while we were working in Florida, Frank got a telegram. "I'm locked in my room on the 28th floor of the Beverly Wilshire Hotel. Need help to get out of here. Swifty." He was looking for a touch.

Frank went to a war surplus store, bought a parachute, and sent it to California with a one-word note: "Jump!"

Probably inspired by this, I played the same kind of joke on Swifty. He was with me when I went into a Miami shoe store and bought my first pair of alligator shoes. "You're such a big-shot comic," he said, "why don't you buy your *friend* some alligator shoes?"

I was in an expansive mood. "Give my father here a pair of alligator shoes," I told the clerk, and Swifty hit me with his cane. He always hit me with his cane when I referred to him as my father. Meanwhile, the salesman was studying Swifty's tiny tootsies—I think he wore a size 4—and whining, "Where am I gonna get a pair of alligator shoes for him? Look at those feet!"

A day or so later, I went into one of those souvenir stores where they sell live baby alligators, and I had one delivered to Mr. Morgan with a note that said, "Make your own."

My father—I'm talking about my real father now, not Swifty—loved Frank Sinatra, and Frank returned the affection. He thought it was terrific that Bernie and I had such a great relationship, because he'd had problems with his own dad. Oddly, Frank's father and my old man looked somewhat alike, they were both little, feisty guys.

When Frank made his Caesar's Palace debut, I was still working the Sands, and my father had just arrived from New York to spend a few days with me. I was going to show him the big time. "Come on," I said, "we'll go watch Frank rehearse."

We walked into the Sinatra rehearsal—the band had been practicing for hours—and Frank still wasn't happy. Finally he said, "Get rid of the second trumpet player, I don't like his sound."

He's opening that night, it's already midafternoon, and he's getting rid of the trumpet player. It was his ear. His ear was uncanny. He sent his private plane to L.A. to pick up another musician, and the rehearsal went on.

During a five-minute break, Frank caught sight of my father. "Bernie," he yelled, "you have to come to my opening."

Bear in mind that Bernie hadn't yet seen my show at the Sands, but I wasn't going to offend Frank. I figured it would work out fine. "Pop, you go to Frank. It's his opening night, he'll only do one show, it'll be over by midnight, and you'll come back to the Sands and catch my second show."

Fine. I reserve a booth for my father. At 12 A.M., I'm ready to go on, and Bernie's not there. The booth's empty, and it stays that way. I come off, it's a quarter to two in the morning, and now I'm concerned. I call Caesar's Palace, get Jilly on the phone: "Where's my father?"

"He's having a ball," says Jilly Rizzo. "Get over here."

I got over there. I walk in, and my five-foot-tall father is sitting in the lounge where Frank's private party is taking place, and he's surrounded by a bevy of beauties, chorus girls who are six foot two, and he's drinking, and smoking his cigar; he's like a pig in clover.

I'm still mad. I walk up to him, and he says, very expansively, "Siddown! Francis will be right back." Francis. All of a sudden, he's such an intimate of Frank Sinatra that he's calling him Francis.

At Frank's seventieth birthday party, I told that story, ending with, "Frank, I've never been able to say this before, but I really want to thank you for getting my father laid." I got the laugh, took my time, waited three beats. Then I added, "And my mother wants to thank you too."

I don't know if my mother would have thought it was funny, but Frank did.

He always said of his own mother that she was his best pal, and when she died, he was devastated. What made it even worse was that she'd been killed in the crash of a plane he'd sent for her. He had a big house in Palm Springs, he'd built the town a Catholic church, and now, when he was grief-stricken, his priest spent many hours with him, trying to bring him comfort. So did a rabbi, a trained psychologist, who was head of a small Palm Springs synagogue called Temple Israel.

If you help Frank, that's a marker, it has to be repaid. He asked the rabbi, "What can I do for you?"

The rabbi didn't want to impose, but Danny Schwartz, one of Frank's closest friends—and a member of the Temple Israel congregation—was more forthcoming. "Frank, they need a Hebrew school for the children."

"Okay," said Frank, "we'll do a benefit, we'll raise money to build the school."

He brought a symphony orchestra to Palm Springs, he got all the local big shots to turn out, and he put on a concert for which he charged maybe a thousand dollars a ticket. He raised a lot of money, and vowed there would be a benefit for the school every year until the temple's building fund had reached its goal.

Some months after this, I got a call from Danny Schwartz. The first anniversary of the concert was coming up, and Frank had instructed him to get in touch with me. "He wants you to do the benefit for the temple."

"Where's Frank?" I said.

"He's sitting here."

"So why the fuck doesn't *he* get on the phone?"

Danny transmitted the message. "He wants to know why the fuck *you* don't get on the phone."

Frank snatched the phone. "What is it? You don't wanta do it?"

"I wanta do it, but don't give me Danny Schwartz, *you* ask me."

"Oh," moaned Frank, "you're a pain in the ass, Alan, you always were such a pain in the ass. I asked you to do me a favor."

"You didn't ask me, Danny asked me."

"All right, I'm asking you now."

It was settled. Frank left Danny and me to work out the details. "Last year, as much money as we raised," Danny told me, "there were such expenses, that big symphony orchestra—"

I interrupted. "I don't need a symphony orchestra, I don't even need a piano. Just put me on."

Danny thought maybe we should have an opening act, and I agreed. "Yeah, we'll get a singer to do fifteen minutes, warm up the place." Danny dutifully repeated this to Frank, who was still in the room, and I heard Frank say, "Well, *I'll* open for him."

That was an offer I could refuse. "I don't want Frank Sinatra to open for me, Danny. This is my night, and I know Frank. He ain't gonna get up there and do two tunes. And even if he *wanted* to do two tunes, that audience is not going to allow it. I am *not* following Frank Sinatra."

Now Frank was on the phone again, like a kid. "Alan! I swear I'll do three, four tunes. I'll bring in my piano player, we save the money for an opening act, and then I'll introduce you. Three, four tunes, that's all I'll do."

I said okay.

Comes the night of the affair, I'm sitting in a big hotel at a dinner table with Frank and Barbara Sinatra and the Walter Annenbergs and the Jerry Fords, who are honorary chairpeople, and I'm dressed in a tuxedo, but I've brought another one along for when I get up onstage. That's traditional in my business; a performer doesn't walk out there with a creased crotch.

Dinner over, I excused myself. I had a suite of rooms upstairs, and I changed, and came down, and Frank was singing. I asked the guy on the door how many tunes he'd done. "About three, four," the guy said.

It was enough. He'd killed the audience, all the people in the ballroom were screeching, "Do another, do more."

So he came back, and started a medley. I marched right down to the stage. "Excuse me," I said. He stopped singing, and began to laugh. "What is it?"

"Frank," I said, "you brought me out here from New York to do this show, and you promised to sing no more than three or four tunes, and now you're in the middle of a medley!"

What a showman. He said, "I'm sorry, Alan," picked up the sheet music from the piano, tucked it under his arm, and stole away. "Ladies and gentlemen," I said, "you'll have to excuse him. Opening acts are all alike, they never know when to get off."

From the dark, in the wings, I could hear Frank muttering, "Crazy bastard."

I could always aggravate him. I'd tell him he didn't know how to make tomato sauce, and he'd go wild. "*I* don't know how to make tomato sauce?"

"Just because you're Italian doesn't mean you know how to make tomato sauce. *I* know how to make tomato sauce."

We once had a tomato sauce–making contest. There were two stoves in the kitchen of his Palm Springs compound, that Italian kibbutz he's only recently sold, and he put up a bedsheet on a rope between the stoves so we couldn't see each other, and when the sauce was finished, he said, "Now we'll have a tasting contest."

So who was tasting? Louie the Light, Willie the Nose, Morey the Mouth. Frank claimed he won, and they all agreed with him, but my tomato sauce was better than his, no matter what his *paesans* said.

I've known him through many domestic changes; I've seen his wives and girlfriends come and go. Ava Gardner was tough. When Frank hit bottom, couldn't get a job, she gave him a hard time.

Then of course he married Mia Farrow at the Fontainebleu in Miami. That's when I did the joke, "He doesn't know whether to bed her or burp her."

Frank wasn't amused.

"Not funny, Alan," he said.

Though he despised the press, Frank considered himself a liberal. I used to argue with him. "You can't be a liberal and want to muzzle reporters. Thomas Jefferson said a bad press is better than a controlled press." He didn't want to hear about it. Today—especially when I find myself cringing at the "scoop" of some so-called investigative reporter—I think maybe he wasn't so far off the mark.

For many years, he was a major fund-raiser for Democratic politicians. He worked hard to elect Jack Kennedy, and at the Armory in Washington, D.C., he produced a preinaugural gala that was amazing. Ethel Merman sang, so did Nat King Cole, Louis Prima, and Helen Traubel. There were appearances by Leonard Bernstein and the Mormon Tabernacle Choir and Nelson Riddle's orchestra. Five actors— Frederic March, Anthony Quinn, Bette Davis, Sidney Poitier, and Laurence Olivier—stood at five lecterns and talked about the significance of the American president in their lives.

And all this on a freezing night in the aftermath of a snowstorm that had left slush and ice on every block in Washington. Ethel Merman's trunk hadn't arrived; she borrowed a dress from Bette Davis.

Frank went out and stood in the snowbanks, helping ladies from their cars.

The evening had two emcees, Joey Bishop and me. Joey did the first act, and I came on for the second. When Joey finished his stint, he introduced me: "Here he is, Alan King." No buildup, nothing.

So I looked at him, and my opening line was, "If I'm a big hit tonight, it's through no fault of yours." After that, Joey Bishop didn't talk to me for three years.

Helen Traubel ended the party by singing "The Battle Hymn of the Republic." It was something to take your head off, it was the entertainment version of the landing on Normandy.

And Frank did it. Everything.

It is well known that Frank came to hate Bobby Kennedy; so much has been written about it there's no need to rehash every detail. But briefly, here's what happened.

In the summer of 1962, President Kennedy was planning a trip to Palm Springs and expected to stay with Frank, who had put in a helicopter pad and strengthened security around the compound. At the same time, Bobby Kennedy, his brother's attorney general, was zealously pursuing an investigation of Sam Giancana, the Chicago mob boss.

The Justice Department felt its probe could be jeopardized if the president continued to fraternize with Sinatra, who was known to be a friend of Sam Giancana. So JFK ended up staying at Bing Crosby's house, which infuriated and hurt Frank. And he blamed Bobby for everything.

Later, when Bobby was running against Hubert Humphrey in the presidential primaries, Frank came out very strong for Humphrey. I was a big Bobby supporter, and one night—fresh from a Kennedy rally—I dropped by Jilly's, a bar and restaurant that was Frank's favorite hangout on 52nd Street. Frank was there, and he was drinking pretty good, and he saw that I was wearing a Bobby Kennedy button on my lapel. He grabbed a Humphrey button from someone, walked over to me, tore the Kennedy button off my lapel, threw it on the floor, and said, "Wear this one."

I'd never been so angry in my life. If it hadn't been that I loved and respected Frank—and that he had two large bodyguards with him—I would have smashed him.

Time went by. I went on campaigning for Bobby Kennedy, Frank went on campaigning for Hubert Humphrey. We hadn't seen each other in quite a while. Then Bobby was assassinated.

A couple of weeks later, I was sitting out in back of my house, looking over Long Island Sound and feeling sad because my son Andy was to be bar mitzvahed the next night, and Bobby wouldn't be there, and in the distance I saw this big old yacht.

It was Frank's boat, the *Tony Rome*, moving toward my house. It couldn't come clear up to the dock, it was too large, and I watched through binoculars as a dinghy was lowered over the side, and three guys got in. They arrived at my dock, Frank, Jilly, Mike Romanoff, and Frank hopped out and approached me. I hadn't spoken a word to him in a long time now.

"I just came to pay a condolence call," he said.

When Frank got older, and was ill, and sometimes did shows that weren't up to his own standards, friends who wanted to be helpful would tell him, "Frank, quit."

This only irritated him. "What do you want me to do?" he'd say. "Put on green pants and play golf all day?"

He came alive on the stage, and he was a lyricist's best friend; nobody could tell the story like Frank. And as he aged, the shows became more emotional experiences. So he cracked on a note—who cared?

The girls of his youth, the ones who sat through six shows a day at the Paramount, wouldn't have cared either. All those little girls, they followed Frank. Frank was an experience.

12 ∽ Confessions of a Political Junkie

Even in dreams, good works are not wasted.
—PEDRO CALDERÓN DE LA BARCA

DISILLUSIONED WITH THE KENNEDYS, Frank (who was, in any case, a friend of the Reagans from the old Hollywood days) eventually became a Republican. Though I never really believed it.

I took my politics from my father. My father voted for Norman Thomas, the Socialist candidate for president, seven times, and I think he only ran three. When Franklin Roosevelt appeared on the scene, Bernie moved slightly to the right. We had two pictures on the wall of our kitchen, Moses on the Mount, and Franklin Delano Roosevelt. My father couldn't decide which one was more important.

Like most kids growing up in those years, I believed Roosevelt would always be president. If you went to Central Casting, you couldn't find anybody to look or act more like a president than he did, with his navy blue cape and his long cigarette holder, and the jaunty way he held his head.

A patrician born, the closest thing to American royalty, he cared about those who hadn't had his advantages. He was the one who saw a third of a nation "ill-housed, ill-clad, ill-nourished," and who pledged himself to a New Deal for the American people.

To this day, I've never voted for a Republican. I'm afraid if I walked into a voting booth and pushed a lever for a Republican, I'd hear my father's voice from the grave, moaning, "Dope, is this the way I raised you?"

My own personal hero in politics—the first one, anyway—was Harry Truman, who became president through an accident of history, after President Roosevelt died in office. Truman ended World War II by authorizing use of the atom bomb, he backed NATO and the Marshall Plan, yet his opponents called him a tool of the Pendergast machine, a hack, and sneered at him for having been a haberdasher. When he ran for a second term in 1948, he was an underdog.

At the time he was barnstorming across the country, making his famous tour, I was in Pittsburgh working at Jackie Heller's Carousel, and I got up early in the morning and went to the railroad station to get a look at him.

Bookmakers were so sure Tom Dewey, the governor of New York, was going to win the election that they wouldn't even take a bet on Truman; the odds were off the boards. But standing to the rear of the platform, back of his train, I could feel the excitement in the crowd that had come out to cheer him on. They were yelling, "Give 'em hell, Harry!" and what this cry lacked in respect, it made up in enthusiasm.

I walked into Jackie Heller's that night, and everyone was talking politics. "I don't know," I said, "I got this strange premonition that this man's going to win," and they all laughed at me.

Even after the election, the *Chicago Daily Tribune* found itself looking silly; an early edition had gone on sale with the headline DEWEY DEFEATS TRUMAN. But I got a nice joke out of it; it went this way: On election eve, Tom Dewey telephoned his wife in Albany. "Put on your finest negligee," he said, "you're going to be spending the night with the next president of the United States." At five o'clock the following morning, Mrs. Dewey called her husband back. "Do I go to Harry's house, or does he come to mine?"

I first met Mr. Truman outside the White House. It was very casual. I was in Washington playing the Capitol Theater with Louis Prima and his orchestra, and we were invited to a party on the lawn, and the president was very charming, even though Louis Prima kept calling him Pops. I took him aside, and said, "Louis, you can't do that, you're supposed to say Mr. President." "Wait a minute," says Louis, "he's the Father of the Country, ain't he?"

Years later, Truman, no longer president, was taking a walk on Park Avenue, striding along with his entourage, followed by crowds of citizens and police. I was one of hundreds on the street near the Waldorf, but, as he passed, our eyes met. He stopped, turned, and signaled me to come over. "I know you, don't I?"

"Mr. President, I'm Alan King," I said. "I'm on television, on *The Ed Sullivan Show*."

No, he said, that wasn't it. "I never watch *The Ed Sullivan Show*, but I know you."

"Well," I said, "a long time ago, I was invited to the White House, and we met, very briefly."

Grinning, he turned to one of his aides. "I'll be a son of a bitch," he said. "And you keep telling me my memory's failing."

We met again at a political fund-raiser. He asked me to sit at his table for a moment, and a captain who was stationed there inquired if I'd like a drink.

"He'll have an Old Turkey," said Mr. Truman. I don't contradict Harry Truman. I said, "I'll have an Old Turkey." "Neat," added Truman. As the captain walked away, Truman turned to me. "Mother is in the powder room, and I'm not supposed to drink, so if she comes back, just keep the glass in front of you."

My favorite Truman story concerns one of my friends, a staunch right-wing Republican named Murray Oliphant. He had become wealthy in the garment business, and every summer, I'd visit him at his villa in the south of France.

Murray Oliphant hated Harry Truman. He called him vile names. If anyone even *mentioned* Harry Truman, Murray would get mad.

Then he had a heart attack, and his wife called me. "The doctor says he should take a sea trip, we should go to France by boat this year. But Murray doesn't want to."

Murray grabbed the phone and I lectured him the way my grandfather used to lecture me. "You'll take the boat, it'll go around Spain, it'll stop several times in the Mediterranean, then let you off in Nice. You'll have eight days, ten days, of salt air, you'll get to your house feeling like a new man."

He was convinced. He boarded the SS *Constitution*, and a few hours later, I got a call from the ship. "You dog!"

"What did *I* do?"

"Do you know who's on this fuckin' ship?" He's braying this over the ship-to-shore radio. "Harry Truman is on this ship. If I could jump off, I would!"

"Serves you right," I said. And I hung up on him.

A couple of weeks later, Jeanette and I flew to France; we were going to meet the Oliphants in Beaulieu. We got to their house, and Murray said, "Sit down. I have to tell you a story." (Before we get to the story, let me offer a bit of background. Like a lot of guys in the garment business, Murray Oliphant never shaved himself. When he was in New York, every morning at eight o'clock, he would go to the Waldorf Astoria barbershop for a shave.)

Now, there were two barber chairs on the SS *Constitution*, one manned by the head barber, the guy who owned the concession, and one by his assistant. Without making an appointment, Harry Truman had gone to the barbershop, and the boss barber wasn't there, so his assistant had cut Mr. Truman's hair.

Murray Oliphant walked into the barbershop while the head barber was chewing out his assistant. "I get a chance to work on the president of the United States, and I'm away from my chair, and *you* cut his hair!"

"What did you want me to do?" demanded the assistant.

"You shoulda called me, I woulda come down!" He was beside himself.

That afternoon, Murray was sitting at a table in a lounge, and Mr. Truman, being a superb politician, and further, being acquainted with someone in Murray's party, stopped by to shake hands.

By now resigned to the fact that he's on a ship with the guy he hates, a guy who's being extremely cordial, Murray decides he's going to behave well too.

"Mr. President," he says, "that was quite a furor you caused in the barbershop this morning."

"What do you mean?" says Mr. Truman.

And Murray tells the story. "The barber's going to kill his assistant—"

Harry Truman listens, picks up the phone, calls the barbershop, and makes an appointment to have his hair cut again—by the boss barber—the next morning.

"That's the greatest gesture I've ever seen," says Murray. "He had his hair cut again! I'm sending a check for twenty-five thousand dollars to the Truman Library."

Adlai Stevenson was another of my heroes, and my best Stevenson story begins—as do many of my stories—with the Friars Club. The Friars were going to honor Jack Benny with a dinner at the Waldorf, and because of my love for Jack, I was on the committee to plan the evening.

Even with his bad toupee, and the crazy uniform hung with medals, we knew Jessel had to be toastmaster. And we knew George Burns would appear, and Bob Hope, and we knew that, at the end, Ted Lewis, with his broken-down top hat and his clarinet, would get up and take Jack by the arm—he always got up and took the guest of honor by the arm—and the music would play, and Ted would go into a sentimental spiel, beginning, "As you walk down life's highways and byways—"

We also wrote a comedy bit for Sophie Tucker to perform, and then we set about looking for a few political dignitaries we could invite. Jack had been in the navy in World War I for about an hour, so we decided to ask an admiral to give him an award, and then somebody mentioned that Jack came from Waukegan. "So let's see if we can get the governor of Illinois."

We looked at each other. "Does anybody know who's the governor of Illinois?" There were fifteen of us in the room, but nobody did. So we called the *New York Times*, found out the governor was Adlai Stevenson, and invited him.

He appeared at the dinner, which turned out to be a memorable event. There was a huge, eclectic crowd of Jack Benny admirers, and at the end, sure enough, Ted Lewis got up and took Jack by the arm, and went into this nostalgic, sad, very sweet speech, and all of a sudden, this old bag lady ran onstage with an umbrella. She was terrible looking, and she was swinging about her wildly with the umbrella, and nobody in the audience knew what was going on. (Even Jack didn't realize for a few seconds that under all that makeup was Sophie Tucker.)

Ted Lewis approached her. "Now one moment, madame," and she yelled, "Don't you call me madame," and hit him with the umbrella. She was trying to get past him to Jack, who was collapsed with laughter.

"What is it you want?" Ted Lewis asked.

She pointed to Jack. "Is his real name Benny Kubelsky?"

"Yes."

"Well, he left me with a duck in the oven."

By now the place was in hysterics, but Ted stayed in character. "Are you implying that he left you with child? That's a terrible accusation. Have you any proof?"

And out of the wings came Jerry Bergen (a midget comedian in a pageboy wig and a Little Lord Fauntleroy outfit), and Sophie Tucker gave him a shot, and he started to play "Love in Bloom" on his violin.

The whole night had gone like that, it was riotous. Fred Allen made a speech in which he said, "I don't understand how they could have an admiral on this dais honoring Benny; he used to get seasick when he heard the Yacht Club Boys."

Fred also talked about the first time he'd met Jack; they'd been on the same bill, he said, in some small town in Tennessee. "The theater was so far out of town it wasn't a theater, it was a cave. The manager was a bear. They didn't have any heat, but they had a fire-eater in the show, and between performances, they used to chase him up and down the aisles to warm the place."

When he'd finished, the audience stood up, en masse. I was sitting on the dais, and I saw Jessel busily rotating a bunch of three-by-five index cards. He realized somebody had to be thrown to the wolves, because nobody could follow Fred Allen. So he pulled Adlai Stevenson's card.

The audience was still buzzing, everybody talking about Fred, when Jessel said, "Now, ladies and gentlemen, the governor of the great state of Illinois, the Honorable Adlai Stevenson."

Nobody applauded, nobody paid any attention; they were still talking about Fred Allen.

Finally, Stevenson got the crowd to quiet down. "Ladies and gentlemen," he said, "I must tell you that Fred Allen and I are old friends." (This, of course, was not true.)

"And," he continued, "I was talking with Fred this afternoon. Now, the Friars have been good enough to supply me with a car and chauffeur, so I asked Fred how he would be getting to the dinner. 'I'll catch a cab,' he said. So I said, 'You know something, Fred? I have a limousine, why don't I pick you up and take you to the Waldorf?' "

The audience was getting restless, wondering what kind of nonsense is this guy spouting.

"In the car," Governor Stevenson continued, unfazed, "I noticed that Fred was quite nervous. 'I have this speech I'm supposed to deliver for Jack Benny,' he said, 'and I just don't think it's good enough.' 'Well, Fred,' I said, 'as governor of Illinois, I have a staff of speechwriters, and it's not important for me to be a hit tonight, it's important for *you* to be a hit. Why don't you take my speech?' So that speech you just heard Fred Allen deliver? That was my speech. And now I'd like to deliver Fred's speech."

The room took notice. You could hear them. "Who is he? What's his name?" He then began to read the dullest speech you ever heard, and every dull line got a scream. When he finished, he got a standing ovation. Just like Fred. Two standing ovations, back to back. I'd never seen that before.

Jessel, standing at the podium, stared out at the audience. "What did you think?" he demanded. "They'd make a schmuck the governor of Illinois?"

I fell in love with Stevenson that night. When he became a national figure, and ran for president, I campaigned for him both times, and never ceased to be awed by his wit.

I got really involved in Democratic politics; I worked for Hubert Humphrey when he was fighting Jack Kennedy for the presidential nomination. I'd met Humphrey when he was mayor of Minneapolis,

---

and did what I could to raise funds for him. Everybody liked Humphrey, even the Republicans.

I was in Wheeling, West Virginia, campaigning for him against Jack Kennedy, and I went on a radio show and made a strong pitch for my candidate.

When I got back to the hotel, Jack Kennedy and his people were just leaving, and as Bobby Kennedy walked past me, he said, "I wish you were on our side." I found out later they'd heard that radio show.

Jack Kennedy beat Humphrey in the West Virginia primary, and Humphrey withdrew from the campaign. Since I was going to work for the Democrat, no matter who he was, I called Bobby Kennedy and said, "I'm ready."

"Glad to have you aboard," he said, and I started working for Jack. Early on, I did a television show in Chicago, and the interviewer asked, "How can you justify the behavior of Jack Kennedy's father? His right-wing thinking?"

"I'm not campaigning for the ambassador," I said, "I'm campaigning for Jack Kennedy."

It was during this period that I met Joe Kennedy, the patriarch. He was a tough bird. He knew my name, but he always called me "young man." Not that we ever had a long conversation. Once Bobby schlepped me along to a strategy meeting in Chicago, and as we were waiting for the elevator, Joseph Kennedy turned to me in front of a dozen people and said, "Young man, you don't approve of me, do you?" I was phumphering, "Ah, ah—" "That's all right," he said, "you approve of my son."

I was very taken by that. I met him several more times in the course of the campaign. He was pontifical, made big statements. One day a bunch of us were talking about power, and he turned to me. "Young man," he said, "the search for power is not evil, it's what one does with power when he gets it that can be evil." I couldn't argue with that.

After Jack Kennedy was assassinated, my relationship with Bobby continued. When he decided to run for senator from New York (he was accused of being a carpetbagger), I was happy to hop on his bandwagon.

I think the reason Bobby Kennedy influenced so many people was that he listened. We'd have meetings, think-tank kind of things, with maybe ten of us in the room, and you didn't have to take what he said as gospel, you could fight with him, everybody fought with him.

Except about abortion. He'd put his hand up—"I don't want to hear it, let's go on." Still, after one meeting, he went to the person who'd introduced the subject. "If you feel so strongly on this issue, put something on paper, and let me read it."

He wasn't a fake, either; he was genuinely concerned with the rights of forgotten Americans. Much later, when he was campaigning for the presidential nomination, he visited an Indian reservation and found the school there had no books on Indian history except for one with a cover depicting a brave brandishing a tomahawk and holding a woman's scalp.

Incensed, Bobby came back to the press plane and started to make a speech about it, but news guys are born jaded; they didn't want to hear it. "Oh, he's starting with the Indians," somebody said, and they all threw their little airplane pillows at him.

He was stronger on civil rights than many of the people in his brother's administration—as attorney general, he'd been instrumental in sending federal troops to Alabama, when Governor Wallace was fighting to keep schools segregated.

On a less exalted level, I too had been involved in the civil rights struggle. Years before, through Harry Belafonte, I'd met Martin Luther King Jr. and was enormously impressed. (Harry and I have been friends for fifty years; I knew him when he was singing jazz at the Royal Roost, before he became a calypso star.)

After the first lunch counter sit-in down South, I went to a Black Freedom rally in Harlem. Harry had invited me, and he introduced me.

The crowd was charged, tense. When I got up to speak, I said, "Why is everybody carrying on about Woolworth's?" and I could feel the room freeze.

I went on anyway. "Have you ever eaten at the lunch counter in a Woolworth's? If you wanted to sit in at the Colony Club, or '21,' I could understand it."

A few people started to laugh, and after that, the anxiety—mine and the audience's—was defused.

1941. My bar mitzvah. Today, I am a man.

The Catskills, above. I made ten dollars a week and stole material from everyone.

Assistant doorman at Leon and Eddie's; on Sunday nights I sang and did impressions.

Havana Madrid Club in New York, the night Jerry met Dean. Seated: Jerry Lewis, Lou Perry, Abe Attel, Georgie Jay, Pat Rooney, Leon Enken, Sonny King. Standing: Dean Martin, me, Pupi Campo.

A surprise birthday party for Jackie Gleason, and what a cast! See if you can spot Art Carney, Gene Kelly, Lucille Ball, and Danny Thomas among those of us surrounding the Great One.

When I wasn't stealing from them, I was playing with them. Here's Jack Carter on clarinet, Jerry Lester on trumpet, me on bass, and Jackie Miles on gourd.

When Judy Garland was good, she was the greatest thing that ever happened on a stage. And when she was bad, she was still pretty good. On one road tour, I got to do "A Couple of Swells" with her.

At a command performance for royalty. Queen Elizabeth said, "How do you do, Mr. King?" and I said, "How do you do, Mrs. Queen?"

I first worked in London because of Judy, and look, I'm so at ease with the high and mighty, I'm introducing Prince Philip to Ethel Merman. (That's Lauren Bacall in the background.)

More travels with Judy.
In Chicago, Cary Grant
came to see our show
every night.
(Here I am with Eva
Marie Saint, Judy, Cary,
and Nelson Riddle.)

Danny Thomas and Milton
Berle changed the way I
worked, but Joe E. Lewis
and Jack Benny changed my
life. That's Joe E. with
Humphrey Bogart, laughing
at my jokes.

Bogart again, with me and
one of my early heroes, Joe
DiMaggio. The year I was
thirteen, Joe hit .381 for the
Yankees.

Miracle in the Rain (1954). I was cast in this movie by accident (the producer thought he'd hired somebody else). Here with Jane Wyman and Van Johnson.

The Girl He Left Behind (1956). I'm the guy in the middle, next to Tab Hunter, but what makes this picture memorable is the extra on the far right. He's James Garner.

The Helen Morgan Story (1957). I got to work for director Mike "Don't give me no motivation, just die" Curtiz (far right) and to play with Paul Newman (center). Walter Winchell, Jimmy McHugh, and Louella Parsons visited the set, and I'm there too, peeking out from behind Louella and Ann Blyth.

I hate Frank Sinatra; my wife has been in love with him for fifty-five years.

With my idol, Jack Benny, at the Tony Awards. He's saying, "Well!"

If Jack was my idol, George Burns was Jack's idol. In Las Vegas, George, Carol Channing, and me. Who said smoking is bad for you?

The cigar again. The guy with the glasses is Swifty Morgan, on whom Damon Runyon based his character the Lemon Drop Kid.

After a few shots on TV with Ed Sullivan, my price doubled. Ed had, as he used to say, "a really big shoe."

How I stayed on the *Garry Moore Show*.

During JFK's presidential campaign, a showbiz political meeting with Adlai Stevenson officiating. At left are Governor Lehman, Myrna Loy, Melvyn Douglas, Anthony Quinn. At right, Betty Comden, me, Jason Robards (half-hidden), Henry Fonda, Lauren Bacall, James Thurber, Maureen Stapleton, Tallulah Bankhead, and, behind Tallulah, Diahann Carrol.

I worked to help elect John Kennedy. Among his other supporters were Shelley Winters and Jane Morgan.

Surrounded by Kennedy
women. At left, Ethel (Mrs.
Robert) Kennedy; at right,
Jean Kennedy Smith, Pat
Kennedy Lawford, and Joan
(the first Mrs. Teddy)
Kennedy.

I first got involved in the
civil rights struggle through
Harry Belafonte, who
introduced me to Martin Luther
King. Here I'm at a rally with
Coretta King and Harry.

When Bobby
Kennedy decided to
run for the senate
from New York, I
campaigned for him.
I thought he was a
real mensch. That's
my wife Jeanette
between us.

More Kennedys. Jackie, Ethel, and Teddy were on hand the day Tony Roche and I, playing doubles, won the Robert F. Kennedy Celebrity Tournament at Forest Hills. I'm still boring people with the tape of that match.

My character in *Just Tell Me What You Want* (1980) was a soul-destroying putz. Here Ali MacGraw smacks me—and I deserved it.

Myrna Loy played my secretary in *Just Tell Me What You Want*. I loved listening to her stories of old Hollywood.

My son, the comedian. I thinl of Billy Crystal as a son, but he's much more than funny. H wrote *Memories of Me* (1988), and it broke my heart, it was so sad. My character was a fai ure who lived in a dream worl that role was my Lear.

I made *Enemies, a Love Story* in 1988. Here I am with Anjelica Huston and director Paul Mazursky. Mazursky captured every nuance of Isaac Bashevis Singer's novel: the wallpaper was right, the actors were right.

Night and the City, starring Robert De Niro and directed and produced by Irwin Winkler. I played an ex-pug and had a prosthesis made for my nose; it looked exactly like my old nose, which I'd broken boxing.

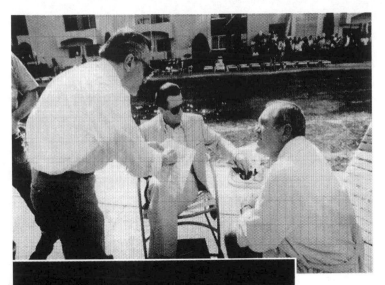

De Niro (again) and me conferring with director Martin Scorsese for *Casino* (1995). I played a teamster controlled by the mob, and died an athletic death.

In the fifties, I played Ensign Pulver in *Mister Roberts* all over the country. Eventually, I got a chance to play Roberts himself, even though my accent was New York, not Nebraska.

A 1965 revival of *Guys and Dolls*. I'd wanted to play Nathan Detroit for fifteen years, and finally got to do it.

One of the few times in
my life I ever listened.
With Arthur Miller and
Laurence Olivier, who said
Brando was the greatest
actor he'd ever seen.

Among my enthusiasms,
Duke Ellington . . .

. . . and Bob Hope . . .

. . . and Barbra
Streisand . . .

. . . and Leonard
Bernstein . . .

. . . and Whoopi
Goldberg.

Because of Harry, who was also close to Bobby Kennedy, I marched from Selma to Montgomery. A bunch of us flew to Selma, and were greeted there by Harry, Floyd Patterson (the heavyweight champion), James Baldwin (the writer), and a bunch of other people, including reporters. One of the reporters asked the actor Gary Merrill, "What are you doing here, sir?" And Merrill said, "I'm not old enough to have been at Valley Forge."

It rained, there was mud everywhere, and Shelley Winters had come in an evening gown and high-heeled pumps. "Why are you dressed like that?" I said, and she said, "Well, I used to wear a long dress at the USO."

As we marched, we were spat on by the National Guard, which was there to protect us (that was when Sheriff Bull Connor came out with his dogs), and the only places that would give us shelter at night were Catholic monasteries, and a couple of shelters run by Irish nuns.

Some of the papers ran slanderous stories saying the nuns cohabited with the marchers, and I made a bad joke about how I'd come down to get a little of that action, and Belafonte grabbed me by the throat. He was not amused.

I remember that Sammy Davis Jr. was frightened; we were all frightened.

The night before we entered Montgomery, Tony Bennett and Joan Baez flew in; there was going to be a rally, speeches and entertainment on some church grounds, but we couldn't get wood to build a stage; lumberyards wouldn't sell to us. Finally, a black undertaker donated some pine coffins, which were nailed together to make a platform.

From Montgomery, we jump-cut. It's 1968. Lyndon Johnson has announced he won't run for reelection. And the day that Bobby Kennedy—in Indiana—begins his own campaign for the presidential nomination, Martin Luther King, who has gone to Memphis to lead a sanitation workers' strike, is assassinated at his motel.

Bobby had just landed in Indianapolis when he heard the news. That night, he spoke on a street corner to more than five hundred black citizens, begging them not to meet violence with violence, especially since Dr. King's life had been dedicated to change that was nondestructive. His voice shook as he recalled the murder of his brother; he said he could feel what many of his listeners were feeling.

Dr. King's death was as shocking as the president's had been, and I thought Harry was going to have a total breakdown; he was on the brink. Julie Belafonte, his wife, phoned me at home. "If you're going to the funeral, please go down a day or two early, and talk to him, somebody has to talk to him." I told her I was on my way.

Meanwhile, Bobby, who had an Eastern Airlines turbojet chartered for the duration of his campaign, sent the plane to Memphis to take Martin Luther King's body home to Atlanta.

The night before the funeral, I attended a meeting in Bobby's hotel suite, along with the black leaders from across the country who were assembled for Dr. King's service. As always, Bobby listened, and asked questions. "What can I do? How can I help?"

We ordered room service, sandwiches, coffee, and talked into the night. To be part of this was one of the most amazing experiences of my life. Next day, an Atlanta paper ran a story that Senator Robert Kennedy had given a cocktail party in his suite the night before Martin Luther King's funeral. Sometimes Frank is right about the press.

I was campaigning for Bobby in Oregon, when he lost the primary there. He was distraught. It was the first time a Kennedy had ever been beaten in a primary. But we were looking forward to a better result in Los Angeles, where a big gala was scheduled. I couldn't stay for the L.A. show, because my son Andy's bar mitzvah was to take place on Saturday night of that week, and I needed to get home; Jeanette was alone, struggling with arrangements.

Bobby had been invited to the bar mitzvah. I'd sent him a wire saying, "Can guarantee you four hundred Jewish votes if you show up." He wrote back, "How many more votes can I get if I come to the synagogue in the morning?"

That was the week he was killed. I heard the news on the radio, and went into the bathroom and threw up my guts. I don't remember this ever happening to me before or since.

We postponed the bar mitzvah party.

I went to St. Patrick's Cathedral for Bobby's vigil, I rode on the train taking his body to Washington, I attended his funeral. It was a desolate time.

The day of the funeral, NBC canceled *The Tonight Show* and asked a group of Bobby's friends to come on and talk about him. We sat at a big round table and tried to answer questions like, "What is the future of politics?" and "What has happened to civil discourse in these angry times?" Whenever there's a tragedy, everyone announces that the sky is falling.

Including me. "I don't know about anybody else," I said, "but I'm finished with politics. They keep killing the good guys."

You wouldn't believe how much mail I got afterward from people saying, "You can't give up, Bobby wouldn't have wanted that."

When I had campaigned for him, I'd taken heat because I was from New York. I'd come into a state and hear, "Why are you telling us how to vote in Indiana?" Or in Oregon, or wherever I was. And I'd say, "I didn't know that good government knew boundaries. I'm not telling you how to vote, I'm telling you how I feel about the country, how I feel about Bobby Kennedy, why I think you should consider him."

I can tell you how I feel about Teddy Kennedy, too. He and I have been pals for a long time. People either love him or they hate him, the way they do all the Kennedys, but even with the problems he's faced— a lot of them self-inflicted—he's still one of the hardest-working senators in the United States. And he may be one of the few voices left in American politics to take up the cause of the less fortunate. He's an ombudsman; he has two offices filled with mail asking for help, and it isn't just from his Massachusetts constituents.

Right after Chappaquiddick, I went up to visit him in Hyannisport. There was a sailboat race scheduled, and the family was insisting that Teddy take part in it. "Come on, we gotta do something." He in turn insisted that I tag along. I'd never been on a sailboat; it was like Rabbi Wise getting on a motorcycle. And there was Teddy screaming at me, "Hang over here!" "Shift your weight the other way!"

When we were crossing the finish line, somebody took my picture. Teddy sent it to me. In the shot, I'm hanging off the side of the boat, and the inscription reads: "To Alan. Because of the events of the past summer, many of my friends jumped ship. I'm glad you decided to hang on."

With all the sorrow, there was also a lot of singing and dancing in that amazing family. One day in Florida, Teddy and I were playing tennis, and he said, "It's Mother's birthday, come have lunch with us." So Jeanette and I went with him to the Palm Beach house, and we walked in, and Rose Kennedy, who was then about a hundred, and wearing a big sun hat, was on her fiftieth lap in the pool.

Through the Kennedys, I lived—up close—a part of American history. I liked the whole clan, but none of the others affected me the way Bobby did. Nor amazed me so often.

He was already a senator when I became involved in a big tax scandal. People close to me, people who wanted to show me how well they were doing for me—my accountants, my lawyer, my manager— were charged with trying to bribe an IRS agent. Next day, the headlines in the papers read, ALAN KING ASSOCIATES IN TAX SCAM.

I was in London, and I flew home, despairing. I was someone who stood on a stage and knocked airlines, knocked doctors, knocked lawyers, knocked the phone company, took the high moral ground on every subject, and here I was accused of income tax evasion.

I went into seclusion in Florida. I was trying to piece out what had happened, pull together the facts, when the phone rang, and it was Bobby Kennedy. "Don't talk now," he said. "When will you be back in New York?"

We made a date for three o'clock the next afternoon at the Carlyle Hotel. The bar is empty at 3 P.M. When we met, before we had any conversation at all, Bobby came to the point. "You have to tell me, are you innocent, or are you guilty? Because if you're innocent, I'm going to help you, and if you're guilty, I'm going to *try* to help you. But don't lie to me."

For forty-five minutes, I told him everything I knew, and everything I didn't know. Soon after that, I went before a grand jury and was exonerated (three of my associates were subsequently convicted), and the whole time, his words were echoing in my ears. "If you're innocent, I'll help you; if you're guilty, I'll try to help you, but don't lie to me." He was a real mensch.

One of his speechwriters, Milton Gwirtzman, said Bobby didn't change, he grew. He was, Gwirtzman said, "always in the act of becoming."

The Kennedys lived on the edge; they were forever racing down rapids, climbing mountains, skiing, playing football. I used to run away from them; I don't do those things. After Bobby died, Ethel sent me a pencil sketch of him that had been used in *Sports Illustrated*. In the drawing, he was wearing a ski outfit complete with mask, and the legend across it read, "Men were not made for safe havens," which had been one of his favorite sayings.

On the sketch, Ethel had written, "To Alan, who was with him for the most exhilarating ride of all."

13 ⌾ Adventures in the Movies

Some talk of Alexander
And some of Fred Astaire
Some like their heroes hairy
Some like them debonair.

—W. H. AUDEN

Making motion pictures—and God knows it's been said before—is probably the most boring art form ever devised. For an actor, anyway. You wait while they hang lights, focus cameras, check sound, tape marks on the floor, and you do the same three lines over and over and over again.

Even so, I like it. I still like to get up at five o'clock in the morning, I like tummling, I like being around it. The action, the action. I can't remember ever being bored. I like the camaraderie, the crazy people.

Back in the fifties, long before I ever stepped in front of a camera, I met Sam Spiegel, who was as great a character as anyone in his movies. Probably nobody in the history of Hollywood produced more crowd-pleasing epics—*The African Queen, On the Waterfront, The Bridge on the River Kwai, Lawrence of Arabia*—and he knew it.

I remember coming out of a theater with him in 1976—we had

been to a screening of *The Last Tycoon*—and on the way to his car, he addressed me plaintively. "The greatest young actor in America today is Robert De Niro, the greatest living director is Elia Kazan, and I may be the greatest producer of all time. How the hell could we make such a bad fucking movie?"

Joe Levine, another fabled producer, was one of my early mentors. When our paths first crossed, I was working clubs in Boston, and he was a film distributor there. In the late fifties, he founded Embassy Pictures, financed artistic Italian films like *8½*, and also brought home to America such schlocky strongman sagas as *Hercules*. He once said, "You can fool all the people all the time if the budget is big enough."

He could even fool his wife some of the time. In New York, he'd bring her to "21"—those were the days when I spent a lot of time hanging out in the bar at "21"—and he'd settle her at a table. Then he'd shoot me a wink. That was my cue to order a shot of scotch.

Joe had gout; he wasn't supposed to touch booze. He'd tell Mrs. Levine he was going to the bathroom, come to the bar, and knock back his shot. Over the course of a couple of hours, this scene might be repeated several times. "My wife thinks I have prostate problems," he said. I laugh, thinking about it. Joe and Harry Truman. Each a giant in his way, but each knew who had the last word in his family.

I never worked for Sam or Joe, though I had some equally eccentric and original bosses. The Hungarian-born Michael Curtiz (who won an Academy Award for directing *Casablanca*) was one of these. A brilliant craftsman, he could not read English; every night his wife would tell him what was in the pages he'd be shooting the next day.

Mike was the last of the European directors to wear puttees and an ascot, and his Hungarian accent was a source of much hilarity. The title for David Niven's autobiography, *Bring on the Empty Horses*, came direct from Mike. It was an instruction he had shouted to a crew when he wanted them to provide him with some riderless steeds.

They tell a story about *Captain Blood*, a movie made in 1935, which illustrates how easy it was to misunderstand a Curtiz order.

Mike was way up on a crane with a big megaphone, and he had a thousand extras milling about, and two galleons rocking in a pool of water (inside, on a sound stage!), and he was directing a big dueling scene between Errol Flynn and Basil Rathbone.

The action was proceeding, crowds talking, laughing, arguing, boats swaying, water rippling, Flynn and Rathbone parrying and thrusting, and in the midst of all this, Mike cued Flynn to deliver the final, killing cut with his sword. "Lunge!" he hollered, and everybody stopped. They thought he'd just called lunch. A thousand extras walked off the set, and Mike didn't know what had happened.

I got to experience Curtiz firsthand in 1957, when I was cast in *The Helen Morgan Story*, starring Ann Blyth and Paul Newman. Newman, who could drink more beer than any man I ever knew, had just come off *Somebody Up There Likes Me*, and he was on his way to becoming a major star, but he was out of the Actors Studio, and Mike Curtiz didn't understand what the Actors Studio was all about. He wanted things done *his* way; when he'd solve a problem on the set, he'd stick out his chest and say, "Dot's why I get the big dough."

Newman and I played Prohibition-era gangsters. For a scene in the Los Angeles railroad yards, we had to run down the tracks at four in the morning (it was freezing cold and misty; Mike had dug a hole and put the camera in it, at track level) and be ambushed by a guy with a machine gun. My character managed to duck around a corner and watch as Newman got shot in the back. Bang! he flew up in the air, and was going through horrific twistings and contortions.

Mike yelled, "Cut!" Then: "What was dot?"

Paul explained. He'd wanted to die in an authentic way; we had a lot of real policemen on the set, so he'd asked one of them, "Did you ever see a man get shot in the back?" "Not with a submachine gun," the cop had said, "but I did see a guy get hit in the back with a slug from a forty-five, and it was comparable to watching him get slammed with a baseball bat."

Inspired by this image, Newman had made his flight into the air. Mike, listening to Paul's spiel, shook his head and muttered. Mike always talked to nobody. He talked, but it was just like he was talking to himself. "How you like this?" he said. "Paul Muni died for me, Humphrey Bogart died for me, James Cagney died for me, Ah-lan Ladd died for me—now this guy's gonna tell me how a man should die?"

Paul was by then doubled up laughing, but he tried again. "Mike, the motivation—"

"Don't give me no motivation," said Mike. "Just die."

I got my acting lesson in another scene. After Newman was shot, I had to telephone Ann Blyth, who was playing Helen Morgan. Helen loved the Newman character, the hustler, con man, wrong guy in her life, and I was emoting, telling her—with fervor—that she'd better get down to see him right away. "I don't think he's gonna make it."

"Cut!" says Mike. "Ah-lan, do me favor. Dunt oct. You personality, not octor. If I want octor, I get Paul Muni."

I drove Curtiz nuts, because of my passion for *Casablanca.* "Tell me about Bogart—"

"Ah-lan, tell me about *Helen Morgan Story,* don't ask me *Casablanca!*" (He always said Bergman and Bogart didn't get along anyway: "He was coughing all over her because he smucked six pox cigarettes a day.")

At one point during the shoot, Newman and I were to swagger into a speakeasy where Helen Morgan was singing. We wore loud suits, and had two beautiful girls, extras, on our arms.

In the script, these girls had no dialogue. The smudge pots were going, the room filled with smoke, the music (provided by Rudy Vallee and his band) playing, the atmosphere was perfect, like a real speakeasy of the twenties, and suddenly one of our dates cried out, "Isn't that so-and-so over there?"

Newman and I looked at each other. Where did that come from? Mike was a great ladies' man; had he made a little gift of a line to this lissome creature?

"Cut!" says Mike, and walks over to the girl. "Dolling, just say very easy, 'Isn't dot so-and-so over there?' "

We start again. The girl says, "Isn't that uh, uh, uh—"

"Cut!" Again Mike walks over to her. "Dolling, just say simple. You know the character's name?" She says yes. "Okay, you walk in, look over, and say, 'Isn't dot so-and-so?' Okay?"

We must have gone five takes, and she blows the one line every time. Ten takes. Newman and I are getting restless, Mike is beside himself, and in front of everybody in the crowded nightclub, the full band, the extras providing local color at the bar, he's talking. As usual, to nobody in particular. "How you like dot? She screws me to get in my picture, now she screws up my picture!"

It was cruel, but it put everybody away. We couldn't stop laughing. That was the end of work for the day.

I left Warners' right after *The Helen Morgan Story*. It didn't mean I wasn't going to do movies anymore, it just meant I wasn't going to be under contract and give up my nightclub career.

And in fact, my club dates fed my later movie work. I was appearing in a London cabaret in 1961, and the producer of a picture called *On the Fiddle* (which in England means on the dole) approached me. He was a Pole named Benny Fisz (pronounced *fish*), whom I'd known since my first trip abroad with Judy.

Benny needed an American sergeant, not unlike Sergeant Bilko, to teach two young English soldiers how to shoot craps. It was a cameo for me, a funny bit. The job took one day, the picture didn't open in America, and I didn't think of it again.

Years went by, five, six, seven years, and I was sitting in the Friars Club when a guy came up to me and announced, "I'm gonna go see your picture at the Paramount."

"What picture at the Paramount?" I said. "What are you talking about?"

"The picture with you and Sean Connery."

"Me and Sean Connery? I never made a picture with Sean Connery, I never even *met* Sean Connery."

"I'm not crazy," he said indignantly. "I just drove up Broadway and there on the marquee, it says 'Sean Connery and Alan King' in some movie I never heard of."

"I know what movies I made," I said. "Wouldn't I know it if I made a picture with Sean Connery?"

By then, he was screaming. "I'm not crazy! I'm not crazy!"

"Okay," I said, and I went out and got in a cab and drove to the Paramount. The marquee carried the surprising news: SEAN CONNERY AND ALAN KING IN *Operation Snafu*. I went up to the theater and looked at the stills in the showcases outside. There we were, Sean Connery and me. He was one of the young guys I'd taught to shoot craps in *On the Fiddle* (which had been retitled for the United States).

Connery was now James Bond, the biggest action hero in America, but in 1961, he'd been a bit player. I'd not only forgotten his name, I didn't remember meeting him. I'd had one scene in that movie, he'd had two, but they were selling the picture as though we'd been the stars.

Here, in chronological order—and positively no other order at all—are some random memories of my life in the movies.

1968. *Bye Bye Braverman.* This was directed by Sidney Lumet. He and I have been friends since our teens, it's like I've known him all my life. He's the kissing director; he kisses everybody. Every time I knew I was going to meet Sidney, I'd brush my teeth. He's a big kisser, and a lovely human being.

Herb Sargent wrote the *Braverman* screenplay (based on a novel, *To an Early Grave,* by Wallace Markfield), about a group of New Yorkers who are trying to find a friend's funeral, and Sidney called me. "Alan, I want you to play a rabbi. In fact, I want you to play two rabbis, an old world rabbi, and then, in a dream sequence, a young, hip rabbi."

The old rabbi was no problem; I had my grandfather to draw on. But in the middle of the funeral service, the old rabbi changes. Instead of a Talmudic seeker after truth ("A man lives, and he dies—is there no time for tears?"), the mourners are suddenly confronted by this sharp young guy speaking in what my grandfather used to call Oxford Yiddish.

And those Actors Studio mourners—Joe Wiseman, George Segal, Sorrell Booke, among others—were daunting. I wanted to look good in front of them, but I couldn't seem to get a handle on the sharp rabbi. Worried, I went to Sidney. "Alan," he said, "you'll do it just the way you do an Ed Sullivan monologue." The minute he gave me that key, I knew what he wanted.

The picture opened, and a reviewer for the *New York Times* wrote, "Alan King plays the rabbi as if he were doing an Ed Sullivan monologue." Sidney telephoned, all excited. "Did you read the review?" "Sidney," I said, "the guy didn't mean that as a compliment."

1972. *The Anderson Tapes*. Again, Sidney Lumet is directing, and I'm reunited with my old costar, Sean Connery. I play a Mafia don (new style, a graduate of West Point), and Connery plays a thief. I think it may have been the first movie about electronic surveillance; Connery is planning a robbery, and he doesn't know his conversations are being taped by the cops.

Looking for money, he comes to me with a proposition. I'm sitting in the Spaghetti Factory, a downtown restaurant on New York's West Side, and I'm dressed as a businessman, and we're talking. I still remember the lines. I tell him I don't like the life I'm leading, hiding behind a legitimate front. "I go home now and worry about my children's school, and if the lawn is nice," I complain. "Man was made for hunting."

I tell Connery I can't give him an okay on the cash he's asking for until I talk to my father. The old man is out to lunch, a vegetable, but nobody knows this, and going to see him will give my character a little more time to consider Connery's scheme.

The script has me arriving at a big estate on Long Island. There a guy, covered with white makeup and attended by two nurses, will be lying on the lawn, and I'm supposed to say, "Old man, you want to die, don't you?" and take a glass of wine and touch it to his lips.

A few days before we're going to shoot this scene, Sidney approaches me. "Alan, can we use your house?"

From that day on, I'd say to people, "You know how I got the picture? I gave him my house."

1980. *Just Tell Me What You Want*. Once more, I got to be part of the Lumet dog and pony show, and this time, I had a lead role. Jay Presson Allen adapted the screenplay from her novel, and while the movie didn't do very well at the box office, it's become a cult favorite. Max Herschel, my character, was a tycoon and a monster. A few years later, this guy would have been a hero, but in 1980—the Milkens and the Boeskys hadn't arrived yet—he was a soul-destroying putz.

I was fifth choice to be Max. I was Sidney's first choice, I was Jay Presson Allen's first choice, but the studio was pushing everybody from Kirk Douglas all the way down the line.

Jay Allen remembers talking to Sidney about the sets, the costumes (they were coproducing, so each of them was wearing two hats), and finally she said, "Why are we beating around the bush? We've discussed everything except our main problem—who's going to play Max?" And Sidney screamed, "I'm *not* going to use Kirk Douglas! I want Alan King!" And Jay said, "What are you screaming about? I want Alan King too."

The only one that didn't want Alan King was Warner Brothers, my old studio, but I didn't know it at the time.

I remember saying to Sidney, "Let's talk about this character." And Sidney said, "He's a guy that eats everything, he never leaves anything in the refrigerator for the next day." That was a part of the character I found interesting; I could identify with it. Nobody likes to eat like I like to eat, nobody likes to drink like I like to drink, nobody likes women like I like women, nobody likes clothes like I do; I understand appetite.

Myrna Loy played my long-suffering secretary, and I had to scream at her all through the picture, using the most foul language. In one scene, I'm plotting to destroy my mistress—beautifully played by Ali MacGraw—because she's run away and married some idiot kid, and Myrna says, "You can't do that," and I'm supposed to bark, "Don't you tell me what I can and can't do! I'll tell *you* what the fuck to do!"

Again, I went to Sidney. "I can't say that to Myrna Loy!"

"You can," he said.

But in rehearsal, I could not spit the words out. Finally, we got on the set, they started rolling, we did several takes, but it was never right. Instinctively, I was apologizing for what I was saying to this great lady. Sidney explained to her why I was having trouble, and Myrna took me aside. "Alan," she said, "don't be afraid to say anything you want. I had five husbands, I've heard it all."

Because of my Brooklyn accent, her name in my mouth became "Moina," and when I addressed her that way, she would correct me gently. "It's Myrna with a *y*, dear boy, with a *y*."

Sometimes, between scenes, she would regale us with tales of the old days in Hollywood, tell about going to soirees at the Gershwin house, about the premieres, the parties, the intrigues, and I would sit entranced, listening to those stories told in that lovely, crackling voice.

Often she reminisced about Bill Powell. When they played Nick and Nora Charles in the *Thin Man* movies, it was the greatest film marriage of all time; they were like Fred Astaire and Ginger Rogers without the music. They danced together, they really danced together.

(Years after *Just Tell Me What You Want*, I met Bill Powell. I was driving through Palm Springs, and I spotted this man in white flannels, blue blazer, blue velvet slippers, and an ascot. He was walking with a dog and what turned out to be a male nurse. Blind by this time, and frail, he was still elegant; he still looked like Nick Charles. He also looked like my uncle Hymie, with his white mustache, white hair, and prominent nose. I got out of my car and introduced myself. "Excuse me, Mr. Powell, my name is Alan King, and we have a mutual friend, Moina Loy." "Ah," he said, smiling, "it's Myrna with a *y*, dear boy, with a *y*.")

When Myrna died, I spoke at her memorial service. I did it without notes, so I don't remember everything, but I know I talked about a scene from *Guys and Dolls*. All these Damon Runyon characters are in a crap game, and they hear that police are coming to raid the place, so they run into a nearby mission, and sit down like members of the congregation. Sister Sarah (referred to as The Mission Doll) is addressing them when a detective walks in. He sees the guys sitting there as innocent as the first day of spring, and he asks Sister Sarah, "How long have these men been here?" "All day," she tells him.

Disgusted, the detective leaves, and in the silence that follows, Big Jule says, "That's a right broad." At Myrna's service, I borrowed Big Jule's words. I said, "Myrna with a *y* was a right broad."

At the same time I was acting with Myrna in *Just Tell Me What You Want*, I was also moonlighting as a producer on a picture called *Cattle Annie and Little Britches*, a family western that starred Burt Lancaster and was being shot in Durango, Mexico.

We were having a lot of logistical problems down there, so I was literally beside myself. Every time I'd get off the set, I'd go right to the phone, call Durango, and talk to my production office.

Sidney found out, and grabbed me. "I'm telling you right now, I don't give a goddamn about your picture in Durango; I only care about this picture we're making here. If I catch you on the phone again, I'm gonna tear it out of the wall!"

It takes a lot to get Sidney Lumet mad, but he was raving, talking to himself like Mike Curtiz. "I've made pictures with Richard Burton and Laurence Olivier. When they finish a take, they go into their dressing rooms, they read, they study their lines. This schmuck is on the phone talking business to Durango."

It turned into a running gag. If I was even a minute late to the set, Sidney would yowl to the crew, "I take a Borscht Circuit comedian, star him in a major motion picture, and the idiot is going to blow it. Somebody get me Henny Youngman."

Get me Henny Youngman. There was a big laugh every time he said it. One day, I wasn't due on the set until after lunch. We were shooting at Astoria Studios in Long Island City, and I had an appointment in New York in the morning. My appointment concluded, I was driving down Central Park South, and there on a street corner stood Henny Youngman. I stopped the car, said, "Henny, come with me," took him to Astoria, sneaked him onto the set, and put him in a closet.

The next scene was to take place in the bedroom of Ali Mac-Graw's penthouse apartment, and Youngman was in Ali's clothes closet. The crew knew it, but Sidney did not.

He came back from lunch, yelled, "Where's Alan?" and the crew yelled back, "Flyin' in." That was their stock answer, "Flyin' in." Sidney roared, "Get me Henny Youngman!" and the closet door flew open, and Henny was standing there, and he started, "Take my wife, please," and did five minutes.

They had to carry Sidney off the set.

We finished the picture, and since Burt Lancaster still had one more scene to do for *Cattle Annie*, I headed down to Durango.

Cattle Annie and Little Britches, played by Diane Lane and Amanda Plummer, are the nicknames of two young girls (the year is 1893) who have come West in search of adventure. Now, having joined up with a gang that's broken out of prison, they—and the felons—are planning to ride through a mountain pass and then blow it up, so that a posse, led by the sheriff, Rod Steiger, won't be able to follow them.

Burt, the consummate pro (he has grown a great full beard), is playing the gang leader, and he realizes that if the girls travel with him and his buddies, they will be drawn into a life of crime, and destroy their lives.

He manages to fix it so they fall off their horses, and before they can remount, the gang has swept through the pass, and Burt has exploded it behind them.

The audience knows the posse is going to catch the girls, but because they're still teenagers, they'll probably be dealt with gently.

So now we've come to the last shot. Burt is standing on the top of a mountain, the girls are stranded on the other side, and he raises his arms and, across the dynamited pass, cries, "Ride with the wind!"

He's releasing Cattle Annie and Little Britches, telling them, "Go."

"Ride with the wind!" That was all we had left to do. We'd already shot the special effects, the explosion, the chase, everything else.

And Burt Lancaster had a heart attack.

We rushed him by helicopter from the mountaintop to Durango where a doctor pronounced his condition stable, and Warner Brothers sent a hospital jet to take him to Los Angeles. My partner, Rupert Hitzig, and I accompanied him to the plane. He was on a gurney, hooked up to an oxygen tank, and as he was being wheeled into the jet, I said, "Good luck, Burt, don't shave the beard."

He always claimed that was his favorite producer story. "I'm dying, and this son of a bitch is worried about matching a shot."

After Burt recuperated, we put him on a mountain in Malibu, got the camera set up, and shot "Ride with the wind!" The mountain was about ten minutes from his house.

14 ∽ FURTHER CINEMATIC ADVENTURES

All of life's riddles are answered in the movies.
—STEVE MARTIN, IN *Grand Canyon*

I STARTED THIS, and I'm going to finish it. So here are still more haphazard, irregular, unmethodical (I own a synonym dictionary) recollections of my career as a movie actor and/or producer.

1981. *Wolfen*. Rupert Hitzig and I coproduced. (I wasn't in it.) It starred Albert Finney and Eddie Olmos, and it was a disaster, a horror story about predatory animals. We used real wolves, and dyed their hair. We had to fence off part of Wall Street to keep them contained while we were shooting, and the Sequoia Club and various other animal rights types picketed us. The wolves were housed on a farm, drinking bottled water, eating good food, living better than the actors, and these people were picketing.

I remember the animals arriving at the location. They came piling out of a van, and their Hungarian trainer rang a bell, like the bell on a child's tricycle, and in response to the sound, the wolves—about ten of them—paraded down Wall Street, and stopped. As I stood there, one of them started to lick my arm. I froze in my tracks. The wolf had my hand, and was licking me, and the Hungarian trainer said, "He's crazy about Rolexes." The sucker was trying to get the watch off my wrist. A terrible experience, that picture, I don't even like to think about it.

1982. *Author, Author!* Al Pacino played a playwright, a real misfit with a houseful of kids, and I played a movie producer.

We were shooting at a legitimate theater in midtown—it was a movie about a play—and because he didn't like the director, Arthur Hiller, Al Pacino was coming to work later every day. (He had just closed in *American Buffalo,* off-Broadway, and he'd been brilliant in it.)

I'd met Irwin Winkler, the picture's producer, and he was hot, having made pictures like *Rocky* and *Raging Bull.* But hot or not, he didn't know what to do about the tension between Pacino and Hiller.

We were having lunch one day, and he said, "You and Al are friendly. Could you find out *why* he's coming in so late?"

It was none of my business, and I knew it, but one morning, when Al arrived even later than usual, I went to his trailer. "Can I see you for a minute?" I said. It's the punch line to a famous burlesque skit that goes like this:

"There's a girl here, there's a girl there. The one with the big boobs is mine, the ugly one is yours."

"You telling me the one with the big boobs is yours, the one with the mustache is mine?"

"Yeah."

Then, with a reverse take: "Can I see you for a minute?"

Any time there was strain on the set, I would butt in, say, "Al, can I see you for a minute?" and he'd break down laughing.

So this time, in his trailer—he wasn't even in makeup yet—I said, "Can I see you for a minute?" and he started to laugh.

"Al," I said, "why are you late?"

He began to rant. "That Arthur Hiller is making me crazy. I'm in every scene, on every page, it's exhausting."

"Al," I said, "how much are you getting to do this part?"

I don't remember exactly what he answered, one million, two million, something like that.

"For three, four, five months," I said, "you did *American Buffalo.* How much did you get?"

"Three hundred fifty a week."

"Was the curtain ever late going up?"

He looked at me. "No."

"When you read this script," I said, "you knew you were on every page. Why are you keeping everybody waiting?"

He laughed. "Nobody ever explained it to me like that, okay?"

But after that, he started coming in on time, and I got flowers and three bottles of Dom Perignon from my new friends, Irwin and Margo Winkler.

Now I'm no longer in the picture. They're shooting the last scene up in Gloucester, Massachusetts, and I get a call from Irwin. "You don't know what just went on. Pacino and Hiller had a fistfight on the dock. It took ten guys to pull them apart, and Al is in the dressing room and won't come out."

"Winkler," I said, "you should have written me into the scene."

1982. *I, the Jury.* A remake of a movie based on the Mickey Spillane novel. Armand Assante played the private eye, and (again) I played a mafioso. Toward the end of the picture, there was a scene set in a big estate on Long Island. (All my mob movies seem to be set in big estates on Long Island, but this time, I didn't have to supply the house myself.) It was supposed to be the headquarters of a bunch of neo-Nazis, ex-military guys who were planning to take over the world. I had arranged to do a deal with them.

So I was driving up to the gate of this estate in a big Cadillac, with Armand Assante sitting next to me and holding a gun to my head, when the neo-Nazis opened fire.

Assante jumped out of the car into the bushes, while I kept driving and screaming, "It's me! It's me!" until the car blew up. There were flames shooting past the windows (gas had been ignited along the path of the car), and there were cameras attached to the car on both sides. By the time I finally got out of there, my pants, the laces on my shoes, my socks, were all burnt, almost to my calf.

After I made my escape, the fire extinguishers were brought in, and as I stood there, heart pounding, I heard the assistant director. (On every picture, the A.D. is the biggest pain in the ass; he's the guy that hollers, "Quiet, we're rolling," and always very loud; they all have terrible voices.) Over his bullhorn, this A.D. was yelling, "We're doing it again, one more take."

"Like hell, you're doing it again," I said. "And if you *do* do it again, there's somebody else going to be sitting in this goddamn car."

When I watched the picture, it scared the hell out of me. My grandchildren saw it on television, and they thought I was a hero. "You really drove that car?" "Sure, I drove that car." They were so impressed, I went on to explain that I always did my own stunts. Go tell grandchildren the truth.

I can still remember my shoelaces smoldering, and the hair on my legs being singed. What a smell. I went back to playing comedy right after that.

1983. *Lovesick.* Marshall Brickman directed, and in the cast were Dudley Moore and John Huston. Dudley ate health foods, and Huston ate like a ravening beast. John would always say to Dudley, "Are you small because you eat like that, or do you eat like that because you're small?"

Huston is one of my great heroes; he was what Ernest Hemingway thought *he* was. (Hemingway used to come into Toots Shor's whenever he was in New York, and one time, Joe E. Lewis told him I'd been a professional fighter. After that, all he wanted to do was arm-wrestle me at the table.)

The ballplayers and sportswriters hung out at the bar in Toots's place. Jimmy Cannon, the deservedly popular columnist who'd worked on the *New York Post* and the *Journal-American*, sat sipping coffee while everyone else got bombed. (He'd quit drinking during World War II, after he'd grabbed somebody's canteen, thinking it was filled with water. The water turned out to be brandy; he'd guzzled it down and almost burnt out his stomach lining.) He called himself "the drunk's best friend," and loved to stir things up.

So did Toots, who was famous for insulting his customers. One night I was at the bar with Huston and Cannon, and Toots accosted me. "Hey, you little crum bum, you never eat here, you only drink here, I don't need your business."

"Why don't you do what I do?" said Huston. "I send Toots a check for fifty dollars a month so I don't have to eat here." For eighteen months after that, I sent Toots a check for fifty dollars a month, and when he went broke, Bill Fugazy and Sinatra and Joe DiMaggio took up a collection to try to bail him out. I said I'd already contributed a thousand dollars.

Huston thought it was the greatest gag. Every time I'd see him, he'd say, "You still sending the bum fifty dollars?"

By the time we made *Lovesick,* Huston had emphysema, and an oxygen tank was always close by. He was playing the head of the psychiatric society (I was playing a psychiatrist), and we were shooting in a brownstone on the West Side of Manhattan. The apartment next door to the set had been rented as dressing rooms and a rest area for the cast, and whenever we'd take a break, I liked to sit and listen to John tell stories. He wasn't as pretty as Myrna, who had also held me spellbound, but he was one of the great raconteurs.

Once in a while, after he finished some reminiscence or other, I'd get up and disappear for a few minutes. (I was a heavy smoker in those days.) At first, Huston didn't comment, but eventually, his curiosity got the better of him. "Where the hell do you keep going?" he demanded.

I confessed. "I'm going outside to smoke."

"Oh," he said, "please smoke around me, blow the smoke in my face." That was before we'd heard about secondhand smoke. I'd blow my cigar smoke right in his face, and he'd beam.

Of course, the way things happen in our business, years later, I made a picture with Anjelica Huston. She adored her father, and we'd swap John Huston stories. I told her we always knew when he was in town—he'd be drinking at Toots Shor's and eating at Luchow's, down on 14th Street. Sunday nights, Luchow's featured an oompah band dressed in short pants, and John had mixed feelings about the noise. "I wonder," he once said to me, "if the food is really good enough to make it worth having to listen to those guys in lederhosen."

1985. *Cat's Eye.* Another mafioso role for me. This time I played the head of Smoke Enders, using Mafia techniques to make people quit smoking. Dino De Laurentiis, the producer, had seen me impersonate wise guys in other movies, and he swore I was Italian.

"No, I'm Jewish."

"Unh-unh. You gotta be Italian, you got every gesture. Maybe your grandfather?"

"No, my grandfather was Jewish, from Russia."

"*His* father?"

He simply would not take my word for it. Except that I got to beat up James Woods (though he usually played crazies, he was the victim in this one), *Cat's Eye* was a miserable shoot. We were working in South Carolina in 120-degree heat, in a studio that had no air conditioning. Dino De Laurentiis. This was big-time movie-making, right?

1988. *Memories of Me.* I've talked about this picture in an earlier chapter, but I have a lot more to say. It was while working on *Memories of Me* that Billy Crystal and I got to be such close friends. Early in the morning we'd sit in the makeup room together, we'd have lunch together, and always, he was pumping me about the past. He's a historian; his love for show business is remarkable.

When I was coming up, I was a monologist. I did my comedy in one, which meant I did it in front of the first curtain. We didn't know from stand-up. And we used to do shows, not sets, but it's the same thing. One morning in the makeup room, I was telling some tale, and Billy cut in. "Don't you know any unimportant people? Everybody you mention is important."

"Would you like me to tell you about my brother-in-law who lays linoleum for a living?" I said. "Most people want to hear about big names."

Billy used to say that every time he'd tell a story, I'd insist on topping it. Well, I've been around longer than he has, I've met more people, I've known seven presidents. It used to drive him wild.

I remember tuning in to *Late Night with David Letterman*, and there was Billy griping about me. "I could never top Alan King," he was saying. "One time, I thought I had him. Since he comes from a whole other generation, I started telling a story about marijuana, and he listened, not saying a word. Finally, I'm through, and Alan gets out of the makeup chair, walks to the door, turns around, and says, 'I only smoked pot once. It was with Lana Turner and Buddy Rich in Norfolk, Virginia.' I threw my makeup kit at him."

When we were doing *Memories of Me,* my father was living in the Hebrew Home for the Aged, in Riverdale, New York. I kept in touch by telephone with the people who were caring for him, and at one point they told me he was very near death, totally catatonic, and they didn't know how long he would last.

I was making a movie about a father, and here my old man was about to take a cab. I decided to fly home over a weekend, and my wife insisted on coming with me; she loved my father. I finished shooting on a Friday night; we took the red-eye and arrived at Kennedy Airport where my car and driver were waiting. It was cold in New York, so I'd asked the driver to bring me a coat. I was going to go straight from the airport to Riverdale.

Let me back up a minute. A couple of years earlier, Jeanette and I were in London, and I saw a vicuna coat in the window of a tailor shop across from the Connaught Hotel. I went in, looked at, touched, and rejected it because it was ridiculously expensive. When I came out without it, Jeanette said I was being silly. "If you want it, why don't you buy it? You don't have to keep worrying about saving it all for the children; get the coat."

So I did. I brought it back to New York, but I could never find a day or a night that was good enough for it, so it never came out of the closet. Until that morning at Kennedy. I must have thirty coats, but my chauffeur had chosen to bring me the vicuna.

In the car, I was cranky about it. "What did you pick the vicuna for?"

"Leave him alone," said my wife. "If he knew from a vicuna coat, he wouldn't be your chauffeur, *you'd* be driving *him.*"

Anyway, we got to Riverdale, and found my father sitting in an atrium with a male nurse. I'd always visited him at least once a week, but I'd been in California on the picture almost two months, and I was shocked at how shrunken he was. This man who had been so strong was just a skeleton, too small in his clothes.

The doctor had tried to prepare me for this, and for the fact that my father wasn't talking, but it was awful. Jeanette started crying, and I said, "Look, this is tough enough, I don't need you crying here. And he doesn't know we're here anyway. Why don't you go wait in the car? I'll sit with him for as long as I can."

She left, and I sat there for maybe fifteen minutes, till I thought my heart would break. Then I put on my coat, and bent over and kissed him on the forehead. He looked up at me and he said, "Nice coat."

They were the last words I ever heard my father utter.

I ran out of the hospital through one of the "Don't Enter" doors, and the bells started going off, and I couldn't stop laughing. I got to the car, and my wife said, "What the hell are you laughing about?"

I told her. "You know what the old son of a bitch just said to me? He said, 'Nice coat.' "

1989. *Enemies, a Love Story.* This was the picture I made with Anjelica Huston. It was based on a novel by a Nobel Prize winner, Isaac Bashevis Singer, a charming man who spoke with a very heavy Polish-Jewish accent. And he didn't want any more of his books being turned into movies because "I didn't like at all what Barbra Streisand did with *Yentl.*"

But in *Enemies,* Paul Mazursky, a brilliant director, captured every nuance of Singer's art. The wallpaper was right, the actors were right. When I saw the completed picture, I could smell the potato latkes cooking on the stove. (Mazursky had been a stand-up comic, and between takes, he and I would fight for the attention of the crew. His favorite line to me was, "Don't you ever *dare* tell me how Sidney Lumet does it!")

I played a rabbi who was more interested in real estate than in my congregation, but making that movie was a great, great joy.

1990. *The Bonfire of the Vanities.* A wonderful cast—Tom Hanks, Bruce Willis, Melanie Griffith—and a bomb. Everyone had thought it was going to be the hit of the century. I'd read Tom Wolfe's book, so I knew the plot, and when Brian De Palma asked me if I'd come in and read for the part of a billionaire who keels over and dies at a table in La Grenouille, I said yes.

When I got to the reading, I heard De Palma—in the next room—having an argument with Tom Hanks. Hanks had grown up watching me on the Sullivan show, and he was horrified that I was expected to audition. "You can't ask Alan King to read!"

Somewhat abashed, De Palma came out to greet me. "Do you *mind* reading?"

"I'm an actor," I said. "I'll read. If I'm wrong for the part, you'll know soon enough."

It turned out fine, but I'll never forget how sweet Tom Hanks was, and how embarrassed.

My death scene went well. I was telling a story to a reporter played by Bruce Willis, and I got hysterical laughing, and dropped dead. The next scene was to be my funeral; they told me I was going to have to lie in an open coffin.

"How long will it take to shoot?" I said.

"Probably two days."

I said forget it. "I'm not lying in no coffin for two days."

Now all the suits converged on me. "You have to do it."

They were paying me by the day at a very nice rate, and the picture had been delayed, so I was making a small fortune. I turned to Brian De Palma. "Do you know how much you're paying me? All you gotta do is make a mask of my face and put it on an extra that's getting thirty dollars a day."

Ooh, they'd never thought of that.

They were shooting in Brooklyn, in the rain, and I had to go into a trailer and get this clay—or whatever it was—smeared all over my face. I'm claustrophobic, so I was not happy, and because it was raining, the stuff wouldn't harden, it never set. The mask didn't come out properly.

Now they moved the location to California. (They had to rebuild La Grenouille out there.) Because they were so far behind schedule, I flew to California to have the new mask made. They told me it was going to be done by a guy who had made the masks for *Planet of the Apes*. "He promises he can get it in one sitting."

Once burned, twice shy; I was nervous—without reason, as it turned out. The guy who'd tried to do the first mask had been a makeup man. This guy was a mask maker. I sat there in a room hung with ape masks, and he made the mold of my face in fifteen minutes.

After the picture came out, people who saw it asked me how I'd felt about lying in a coffin. "Oh, I'm a pro," I'd say. I never admitted the body in the coffin belonged to some poor guy wearing my face.

1992. *Night and the City*. Irwin Winkler was producing, and he wanted me for the part of an ex-pug, a gangster–fight promoter called Boom Boom. This time, I would get to play a *Jewish* mafioso, in a movie starring Robert De Niro. Though De Niro knew me, he wasn't sure I was right for Boom Boom, and Irwin came to me, embarrassed. "Bobby loves you, but he's a little afraid—"

I knew instantly what this was all about. I'd lost several parts in pictures because some people thought I was too well known as a comedian and might not be believable as a different character.

"Would you come down to Tribeca and meet with De Niro?" Irwin said.

I agreed to the meeting, and prepared for it. I found the guy that did the nose for Tom Cruise in *Far and Away*, that picture where he played a bare-knuckles fighter from Ireland. The nose maker came to my office, and he put this fighter's nose on me, and turned me into what I thought Boom Boom should look like. Then I put on one of my old Nathan Detroit *Guys and Dolls* suits, and went downtown.

I sat with De Niro for half an hour, and he never noticed the nose. Finally, he said, "There's something different about you."

"For an actor, you're very observant," I said. "I sat for two hours to have this prosthesis made, and you just see 'something different' about me?"

We shook hands—I was in the movie—and I went out and stood and waited for a cab while passersby yelled, "Hi, Alan." My disguise didn't disguise me for a minute. After we'd finished *Night and the City*, I looked at the stills and realized the nose I'd worn for the picture looked exactly like my old nose, which I'd broken boxing, and which I'd had fixed right after *The Helen Morgan Story.*

1994. *The Infiltrator.* I went to London to play someone I knew, Rabbi Marvin Hier, who's dean of the Simon Wiesenthal Center for Holocaust Studies. And I got to do a wonderful confrontation scene, making a speech to the new German government, accusing them of pushing under the rug material about present-day Nazis. The script has Rabbi Hier considering the leaders of new Nazi splinter groups. "Get one of them," he says, "and the others don't sleep so well."

1995. *Casino.* Martin Scorsese directed, with De Niro, Joe Pesci, and Sharon Stone, and I relived my youth, because *Casino* is all about the last of the wise guys in Vegas. The character De Niro plays is based on a guy called Lefty Rosenthal, who now owns a bar in Florida and has been living—or trying to live—a very quiet life.

But as soon as Scorsese started making this movie, there were stories about Lefty Rosenthal in all the newspapers. I read a front-page account of his life and was fascinated. I mean, hoods blew this guy up in a car, and he survived.

So one day, finding myself in Boca Raton, I went to his bar and had a drink. There was a big fat barmaid working, and I asked her if Lefty was around.

"Why?" she said. "You read that story in the papers? Everybody's comin' in here because of all this stuff in the papers. He left town because of all this stuff in the papers."

I was finishing my drink when somebody at the bar recognized me, which piqued the barmaid's interest. "You Alan King?"

"Yeah."

"You in this picture where Robert De Niro plays Lefty?"

"Yeah."

"Robert De Niro shouldn't be playing him," she said. "Richard Widmark should be playing him."

Richard Widmark's eighty years old now, but everybody's a casting director.

The best thing about making a movie with Scorsese or Lumet is that they love actors, and there's nothing better for an actor than working with a director to whom you're not just a piece of meat.

You have discussions, you spend time improvising. Scorsese will let you do the shot one way, then try it another way. It gives you such a feeling of being part of the picture.

Marty wanted to hear all my stories. I'd known these mobsters in the sixties and seventies, which helped because I was playing a teamster boss who was controlled by the mob.

It was a hard shoot. Nights in the desert, cold and rainy. I traveled back and forth between Vegas and New York, but Don Rickles, playing a casino manager, was out there for five months. And even when he was off camera, he was onstage. He insulted everybody—"Bobby De Niro! World's greatest actor, can't even walk, look at this man!"—and kept everybody laughing, which boosted morale.

After his last scene, when he wrapped, the cast and crew opened champagne and applauded for ten minutes. I'd never seen anything like that, even crazy Rickles had a tear in his eye.

In my own final scene, I was shot down coming out of a restaurant. There was fake snow on the ground, and Marty gave me instructions. "You walk out of the restaurant, you move toward your car, two guys come from behind the car, one puts a gun with a silencer to your head, and bang, bang, down you go. Then they administer the coup de grâce, shoot you while you're lying on the ground, lying between two cars."

The plan was for me to get to my mark beside the car, and as soon as the guy put the gun to my head, Marty would cut. Then he'd go for a long shot of the killing, with a stunt man substituting for me, jumping around, hitting the cars, dying a very athletic death. (Mike Curtiz would have hated it.)

They'd put the stunt double in clothes just like mine; it was like I was looking into a mirror. But I'd been framed, and I never saw it coming. Marty took me aside. "Alan, do you think *you* could do the fall? Because if I could get this in one long shot, it would be much more effective than cutting."

"Let me try," I said.

Now they got rubber pads for my knees, my elbows, and me being a ham, arthritis or not, sixty-seven years old or not, when I was shot, I died like a little kid playing cops and robbers, hitting one car, then another, until I fell down.

"Great," said Marty. "Let's do it again."

My suit had fake snow all over it, I had to change clothes. We did nine takes, with me falling, and at the end of each take, Marty said, "One more time."

After the ninth fall, I rebelled. "No more times, Marty. Maybe instead, you'd like me to drive a burning car?"

They sent a masseur to the hotel, I sat in a hot bath (I'd hurt my back), and the insurance company called and wanted to know if I was injured. "I'm fine," I said. "I may never walk again, but I'm fine."

And Marty was right. It was a much more effective scene than it would have been if he'd had to cut.

15 ∽ On—and Around— the Boards

The art of acting consists in keeping people from coughing.
—SIR RALPH RICHARDSON

IT'S TRUE, I've done more movies than plays, but I've worked harder on plays.

I've referred to my early stage work (my acting stints in *Mister Roberts*), and I've also mentioned my old Nathan Detroit suits, but up till now, I haven't mentioned Nathan Detroit. Nathan is the gambling man who has been engaged to a nightclub singer–hoofer called Miss Adelaide for fourteen years; they are both characters in *Guys and Dolls*, a musical comedy that first opened on Broadway in November of 1950, at the 46th Street Theatre.

I was in the audience that opening night. Sam Levene, one of my favorite actors, was barking his way through Nathan's lines, and I turned to Jeanette. "Someday," I said immodestly—because Sam Levene was peerless—"*I* want to play Nathan Detroit."

At twenty-three, I wasn't ready; fifteen years later, there was no problem; I made a career out of Nathan.

When, in 1965, we did a revival of *Guys and Dolls* at City Center,

158

a reviewer for the *New York Times* said, "Alan King plays Nathan Detroit as if he had never seen Sam Levene." That was one of the few reviews I've ever enjoyed.

Frank Loesser came backstage and told me that when he'd written the music for the show, Nathan had had four songs, "but Sam couldn't carry a tune in a barrel, so we had to keep taking songs away, and he ended up with nothing but 'Sue Me,' which he talked."

There was a little piano in my dressing room, and Frank proceeded to sit down and play me all the songs they had taken away from Sam Levene. And I felt awful, because I could have sung them.

For a long time afterward, whenever I had a free week or two, I played Nathan Detroit somewhere. Or directed *Guys and Dolls* somewhere. I directed Tony Martin as Sky Masterson, in a touring company. At first, I turned down the job; I told the producers I really didn't have the time, but Tony called me. "You owe me, Alan," he said.

I made the time. We were to open outside of Boston, at a theater in the round. During rehearsals, for two weeks, Tony and I were roommates, and I jawed at him constantly. He wasn't one of the great actors, but nobody looked better in a striped suit and a dark shirt and a white tie than Tony Martin; he was born to play Sky Masterson.

"But," I kept saying, "you got to remember Sky is not Tony Martin. He's not an entertainer, he's a hard-nosed gambler."

There's a scene in the script where Sky, who's crazy about the Salvation Army worker Sister Sarah, asks some fellow gamblers to come with him to a meeting at the mission. Lowlifes all, they greet this request with cries of "Get out of here!" and Sky has to come up with another proposal. He'll roll the dice for their souls. If he wins, they appear at the mission; if he loses, he pays off in cash. This is the point at which he picks up the dice and launches into the song "Luck Be a Lady."

"Tony," I say, "this is the big moment for Sky. Don't even *sing* the verse, talk it. Look at the dice, the dice are like a woman, and talk to them. 'They call you Lady Luck, but there is room for doubt—' " I go at him, and at him and at him, and he's listening, and doing the words brilliantly.

Four nights before the opening, Cyd Charisse comes to Boston, and I move out of Tony's room so she can move in. Opening night, I'm standing at the back with the producers, and I say, "Wait till you see Tony, he's wonderful. Wait till you hear him get ready to do 'Luck Be a Lady.' "

The moment comes. He talks the verse—"They call you Lady Luck—" and he's great, focused. Then he gets to the chorus, and as sure as there's a God above, he starts to croon. He's standing there, one hand across his belly button, and he has one arm extended, and he's doing this kind of box step he used to do when he sang in nightclubs; before my eyes, a tough guy is turning into a lounge lizard.

I ran out of the theater, got in my car, and drove back to New York. I never saw the rest of the play.

In the fall of 1965, a wonderful gentleman named Walter Hyman came to me with the script of a play called *The Impossible Years*—a comedy about a psychiatrist who writes a book on adolescence but doesn't comprehend the first thing that's going on in his adolescent daughter's head—and invited me to coproduce it with him and David Black.

I took him up on his offer. I'd never produced for Broadway, but I'd been doing all my own television specials. It started when I was working on a special for Timex and getting a little unhappy with the way it was being done, so I complained to the ad agency. They said, "Well, why don't *you* produce it?" That was the story: All right, smart guy, *you* do it.

Few people in the business thought *The Impossible Years* had a chance—so few, I invested $25,000 of my own money in it, and also took on the lead role—but it ran for 670 performances. I left after a year and a half, and was replaced by Sam Levene.

I had created the role, I'd played it on Broadway for a long time, so there were actors who just didn't want to follow me, but following me didn't bother Sam a bit; other things did. Usually, a stage manager goes over the show with a replacement. Sam balked. "I'm not having any stage manager direct me, I want Alan." Because I was anxious for everything to proceed smoothly, I ended up directing Sam.

He was a tough old codger, but when I had to deal with someone who had a tough reputation, I would kill that person with love. How can you hate a director who keeps telling you, "You're the greatest, you're the best"?

I rehearsed Sam for two weeks, and one day we had a big fight, and he walked out on me, squawking, "What do *you* know? You're a nightclub comedian! A Catskill comic!"

I went out and bought him a beautiful coin in a velvet box (he collected medals and coins) and next day, I came to rehearsal with it, and when Sam appeared, he couldn't believe it, he'd thought I was going to kill him.

"Look," he said finally, "don't come to my opening night; in fact, don't come to see me for a week."

"Sam," I said, "I was in this play for a year and a half. I had a calendar on the wall, and I marked off every day like I was in jail. There's no reason I'd want to come back to see you or anybody else in it. I swear I'm not going to come for a week."

I was still playing the show at night and rehearsing Sam during the day, and the first night I was free, the night Sam opened—it was a Monday—Walter Hyman gave me a dinner party at the Colony Club. There were maybe a dozen guests, and we were sitting there having cocktails at 7:30, and I kept looking at my watch. It was the firehorse syndrome. In those days, the curtain went up at 8:30.

At about eight o'clock I couldn't sit still anymore. "Walter," I said, "let's get in the car—we'll leave everybody here—and go to the theater. I just want to see Sam's entrance."

We drove to the theater, looked at our watches, waited outside until we knew the house lights had gone down to half. Then we went in and stood at the back of the orchestra. All the little lady ushers with the white lace collars came running over—"Oh, Mr. King, Mr. King"—and I was saying, "Shh, don't tell anybody I'm here," when the curtain went up.

Sam made his entrance down a flight of stairs—the character had a big hangover—and got his first big laugh, and I said, "Okay, Walter, let's get out of here," and we returned to the Colony and the dinner party.

A week later, I went back and caught the entire performance. I strolled backstage afterward, and Sam opened his dressing room door.

"You lied!" he snarled. "You were here last Monday night." An usher had turned me in.

At some point during the run of *The Impossible Years*, in a theater right across the street from The Playhouse (where we were installed), a drama by Howard Da Silva was about to open. Da Silva was better known as an actor, but he'd written this play called *The Zulu and the Zaide* (Zaide is the Yiddish word for "Grandpa"); it starred Menasha Skulnik and Louis Gossett Jr.

They were in previews, and they had a big advance. I hadn't seen the show, but I was standing outside before it opened, and along came Howard Da Silva. "You know," I said, congratulating him on his business acumen, "with Menasha, the darling of the Yiddish theater, you should be getting every Jewish organization and theater party in the city."

Howard, who could be terminally pompous, took offense. "This is not a Jewish play."

"Oh yeah?" I said. "How many Zulu theater parties are there?"

He never spoke to me again.

Here's the worst thing that happened while I was still acting in *The Impossible Years*: I was backstage getting dressed, and I heard a big commotion out front. Lights were about to dim to half, and my partners were hanging around in my dressing room. They were there every night, but they didn't have to stay; once the curtain went up, they could march across the street to the bar, and pretend they were still working. That delightful lifestyle was one of the reasons I started producing on Broadway, but it didn't do me too much good with *The Impossible Years*. Even though I was an equal partner, I had to be onstage for two and a half hours, while these guys were sitting in the Absinthe House.

But getting back to the commotion, we soon discovered what was wrong. The stage manager came in to report, "Somebody dropped dead in the theater."

The dead man was lying in the aisle where he'd fallen, and nobody could touch him. That was the law. Nothing could be moved until the police and the ambulance came. And they didn't show up for half an hour.

I was shaken. I looked through the curtain and saw a body on the floor, and I was expected to go out there and play a comedy. The furor quieted down, the body was removed, and I turned to my partners. "Give everybody their money back, I'm not going on."

"Alan," one of them said, "it's standing room only."

I said no, they said yes. "Nobody in the audience has moved, they're waiting for you."

"Tell you what," I said. "I'll go and talk to them."

I put my dressing gown over my wardrobe, and walked out in front of the curtain. I couldn't believe it, people were applauding. "Ladies and gentlemen," I said, "I don't have to tell you that a tragedy has just taken place in this theater, a man has lost his life. Do you think it's appropriate to play a comedy now? Do you want this curtain to go up?"

Oh boy, did they. They were whistling, clapping, calling, "Curtain up!"

I couldn't believe it. I looked out at them and said, "I refuse to perform before such an uncaring audience. The show must go on? Bullshit."

Still in my robe, I marched offstage, across the street to the Absinthe House, and proceeded to get drunk, and the box office had to give everybody their money back. Those people were like animals! They didn't give a damn. And my partners were chasing me, yelling, "People came all the way from Wilmington."

It was a terrible, terrible night.

Soon after my experience trying to appease Sam Levene, I had to try and placate Rosemary Harris. This time, Walter Hyman, Gene Wolsk, Manny Azenberg, and I were producing *The Lion in Winter*, which starred Robert Preston as Henry II of England, and Rosemary as Eleanor of Aquitaine, his wife. I used my "You're the best!" technique on Rosemary. I sent my car and chauffeur to bring her to the theater for rehearsals, and every day, because she loved champagne, I had a split chilled and waiting for her in the backseat.

Everything was fine until we opened. Then she started breaking everybody's balls, including Robert Preston's (though he was always a total gentleman), and chewing the scenery. I finally had to go backstage and read her the riot act. "You ought to be ashamed of yourself,"

I said, and she began to scream at me, and I screamed back at her, and we screamed it out pretty good.

She later gave an interview to the *New York Times.* "Alan King is the greatest producer," she said. "During rehearsal."

A few months after *The Lion in Winter* opened, I coproduced (with Walter Hyman, Elliot Martin, and Lester Osterman) *Dinner at Eight*, at the Alvin Theatre. It was a revival of the Kaufman-Ferber play first done in 1932. It was also an accident. Here's how it came about.

I had received a script from a writer named George Lefferts. It was called *The Boat*, and it was right after some English guy had got into a boat and sailed around the world, and been knighted by the Queen.

I thought Lefferts had written a powerful story about a man who had a dream. The protagonist owned a small delicatessen in the Bronx, and in his backyard, he was building a boat. It was a symbol of his yearning to escape his life, but you knew he would never finish it; he would never get it out of the backyard.

Edward G. Robinson had just closed in *The Middle of the Night*, the Paddy Chayefsky play; he was weary, and he was going through a difficult divorce. But he and I were longtime friends, and I'd meet him after the theater, have coffee or a glass of wine with him, trying to get him to commit to this play. Because he loved the script, but he kept saying no. "Will you stop hocking me with this boat already? I'm a tired old man, leave me alone."

Then one night, after a couple of red wines, he said, "I'll do it on one condition. You get Tyrone Guthrie to direct."

I knew from Tyrone Guthrie like I know from the Sultan of Brunei. But I promised Eddie I'd get the director he wanted. I initiated a correspondence with Guthrie, who lived in Ireland, and asked him if he'd be interested. He wrote back: "Send me the play."

I said to Walter Hyman, "We're going to deliver the play to him by hand." Walter hated to fly, but I convinced him this would be a coup. "Another *Death of a Salesman*. Think about it, starring Edward G. Robinson and directed by Tyrone Guthrie!"

He thought about it, and he flew with me to Shannon. We went to Guthrie's farm in Limerick, and it was wonderful. So was Guthrie, an enchanting man, a huge, imposing man. He was six foot six, and like a lot of big men, he had bad feet. He walked very gingerly.

We sat there in his living room while he read the play, and then we all went out to dinner. He couldn't have been more gracious but he said he just didn't feel he wanted to do the play. I was very disappointed, and next afternoon, as we were preparing to go back, we stopped by his place to say good-bye. We were just walking out the door when I turned around and said, "Excuse me, is there any play you *would* like to direct?"

Walter grabbed me by the arm and started pulling me outside, muttering, "What do you mean, is there any play he'd like to direct?"

"Wait a minute," I said, peering back hopefully. Guthrie looked at me. "Yes," he said, "there is a play I'd like to direct."

We missed our plane. We turned around and sat down. Guthrie announced that he wanted to do *Dinner at Eight*. He'd always been fascinated by the movie version. When Walter got me alone, later, he hit the ceiling. "Why do I want to do a revival of *Dinner at Eight*? Who gives a damn? What the hell is the matter with you anyway? You're going to let him pick a play to do on Broadway?"

I said yes, I was. "I want to be able to tell my grandchildren that I produced a play directed by the great Tyrone Guthrie."

I put on my producer's cap and started working. "We'll assemble an all-star cast, like they did in the movie. They had Marie Dressler, John Barrymore, Lionel Barrymore, Billie Burke, Wallace Beery, Jean Harlow—that's what we'll do, it will be a revolution on Broadway."

"How are you going to get anybody to commit?" Walter said.

"We'll keep changing the stars," I said. "If they want to play six or eight weeks, we'll let them come."

We got it together. We had June Havoc to play the Billie Burke part, Walter Pidgeon to play the Lionel Barrymore part, Arlene Francis to play the Marie Dressler part. It was a wonderful cast. And we decided not to take it on the road, we'd just rehearse in New York, and open. We had offices on 55th Street, and Guthrie was over at the Amsterdam Theater with the cast. The Amsterdam Roof was being used as a rehearsal hall.

I wanted to see it all happen, so the first day of rehearsal I told

Walter I was going over to watch. "I'm not going to interfere in any way, I just want to see Guthrie direct."

It was such a large company—there were twenty-five people on the stage at one time—and the rehearsal was a disaster. Guthrie sat in the audience, said a few words, and then everybody moved around the stage, and some of them were reading out of scripts, and I was thinking, I don't believe this. But I wasn't about to go back and tell my partners I had just witnessed a catastrophe. I returned to the office, they asked, "How's it going?" and I said, "Guthrie's a genius."

Next day, I ran over there again. It was worse than the first day. Guthrie never stirred, and pandemonium reigned. All of these actors had seen the movie, and they had preconceived ideas of how to play the parts, and Guthrie never said a word, or offered a single suggestion, just sat in the middle of the dark theater. For four days. And I was hanging out in the back going nuts. I finally decided I had to do something. It was a zoo up there.

Without telling my partners, I went over to Guthrie's friend—he was a Russian, Guthrie's manager and confidant—and said I'd like to take the two of them to lunch. Then I made a reservation in an Argentine steak house on Broadway, right up from the Alvin. I got to the Amsterdam Roof about an hour before lunchtime, and the actors were going through the big dinner party scene, and it was horrible.

Finally, June Havoc, a great broad, stepped down to the foots and screamed into the dark, "Tony, when the fuck are you going to start directing this play?" And at that cry from the heart, this giant man stood up in the dark, walked up the ramp to the stage, took off his jacket, turned to a cast of thousands, and said, "Ladies and gentlemen, I think now you are all ready to be directed."

In five minutes, he brought order out of chaos. "You come down the stairs, you go over there, you do this," and I'm standing in the back with my mouth open.

Lunch was called. Guthrie, the Russian manager, and I started down the street on our way to the steak house, though I realized our conference was no longer necessary. And as we walked along, Guthrie spoke. "Vaudeville"—he used to call me Vaudeville—"I'll bet you were wondering how I was going to control this pack of so-called stars."

He was so wily, so cunning. He wanted them to bury themselves, to get into trouble so deep they couldn't dig themselves out. Then, when he finally started talking, they wouldn't talk back.

We opened on September 27, 1966.

In 1966, I was a very busy boy. *The Impossible Years* (although it had opened in '65, it was still going strong), *The Lion in Winter, Dinner at Eight*, and I wasn't done yet. I also coproduced *The Investigation*, by Peter Weiss, the German playwright who had written *Marat/Sade*.

A drama drawn from the court records of the trials of guards and officials at the Auschwitz concentration camp, it was the most traumatic thing I've ever gone through in the theater. Or anywhere else, for that matter.

It had been three hours long when it played in Germany—we cut it down—and Ulu Grosbard, who, with Jon Swan, did the English translation, also directed it here.

It was so emotional, actors were fainting on the stage during rehearsals, and even in performance. We opened in the Ambassador Theatre, to tremendous reviews, but it wasn't the kind of play people want to go see for a night on the town. We kept it open anyway, and let high school kids come in for a dollar.

Sometimes, people would walk out in the middle, and I'd be standing in the back, and they'd recognize me, and they'd say, "Why are you doing this?" And I'd say, "Why are you walking out?" and they'd pull up their sleeves and show me the tattoos on their arms. "We don't have to live this again."

It was tremendously controversial. During previews, we invited a lot of rabbis and a lot of Jewish organizations to come and see it; we wanted to know if we could really open it. After the play, we'd have debates on the sidewalk, under the marquee, pro and con.

Listening to the actual testimony of Auschwitz survivors and their torturers made your blood run cold. At the end, there was no curtain, the stage just went dark, and you couldn't hear a sound in the theater. People always talk, comment, but not at this play.

One night, Sidney Lumet was standing at the back of the house with me, and I said, "Wait till you hear this, when it's over, there's no noise, no applause, nothing, you just hear the feet of the audience leaving."

"It sounds like the shuffling of the prisoners," he said, "as they're marched into the gas chambers."

It was a terrifying experience. When we closed, we found we had a $25,000 profit, and my partners and I looked at each other. "What are we going to do with this?" Then we read that Simon Wiesenthal, the Nazi hunter who had just written a book called *Murderers Among Us*, was visiting New York, staying at the Algonquin Hotel. So we invited him to lunch and gave him a check for $25,000 to be used for the work of the Simon Wiesenthal Center.

Now, almost thirty years later, I'm seriously thinking of returning to Broadway. Already I've called some of my old associates and asked them to update me on the theater. And you know something? Nothing's changed. The breakdown's still the same, the writers get this, the composer gets this, the backers get this, nothing has changed except the costs, which are now almost prohibitive.

My wife believes I'm demented. During production in the old days, when I was going through a difficult time, and I'd be up half the night, she would say, "What do you need with this?" And I'd say, "If I didn't need it, I wouldn't do it." The action was something I craved. I still do.

16 ❧ WHERE HAVE YOU GONE, JOE DIMAGGIO?

They were swifter than eagles, they were stronger than lions.
—BOOK OF SAMUEL

THE YEAR I WAS thirteen, Joe DiMaggio hit .381 for the Yankees. He could whack any baseball that came his way, and he also led an exemplary private life. But even if he hadn't, we wouldn't have known about it. Back then, there was a kind of unwritten law among sportswriters; they didn't rush to expose every big leaguer who tippled, or was nasty to his mother.

It's different now. Journalists build up athletes just so they can knock them down again. They take a Michael Jordan, make him a giant (though I guess we'd have to say God preceded them in that particular effort), then get self-righteous when they find out he went with his father to play cards in Atlantic City. Who the hell cares?

Were the champions of my youth better athletes than the champions of today? I don't think so. But we were allowed to admire them in peace.

Sports played an important part in the lives of most of my generation. I know I'm sounding like an old man (which I am), but when Sinatra sings a Joe Raposo song called "There Used to Be a Ball Park Here," about a place like Ebbets Field, home of the Brooklyn Dodgers, I can't listen to it without getting all sad and nostalgic.

My own career as a jock started with stickball in the streets of Brooklyn. I was a two-sewer guy. The court was marked off by sewer covers; if you could hit two sewers, that was a big thing. You'd use a cut-off broomstick for a bat, and you'd hit a Spaldeen—a little rubber ball made by Spalding. We played hockey on roller skates too; the streets were our arena. Kids today sit down with a computer and Nintendo—not us, we kept moving.

One of my early heroes was Satchel Paige. Because of the color bar, he played baseball for twenty-two years before he ever made it to the major leagues, though he was such a good pitcher that in one exhibition game, he struck out Rogers Hornsby (then the National League Batting Champion) five times. In 1926, Satch had begun pitching for the Black Lookouts, of Chattanooga, Tennessee; after the Lookouts, he played for the Birmingham Black Barons, the Nashville Elite Giants, and the New Orleans Black Pelicans. He even pitched for the Colored House of David team (they all had long whiskers, and they gave him a fake red beard).

I saw him in action with the black teams. I once watched him pitch two complete ball games in a single day, and one was a no-hitter. It shouldn't have surprised me; back in 1935, he'd pitched every day for twenty-nine days.

It wasn't until 1948 that Bill Veeck, a big showman (he once hired a midget to go up to the plate and get a walk), finally signed Paige to play for the Cleveland Indians. Nobody really knew how old he was at the time, but he helped the Indians win the World Series that year.

I remember I was working at a theater-in-the-round in Phoenix when the Indians were there for spring training, and I wanted to meet Satchel Paige, so I went out to the ballpark. He was very smart, witty, very down-home, as rural as you could get in his humor. We chatted, we had a cold drink, I watched the players work out, and at the end of the day, Lou Boudreau, the team's manager, called, "Okay, two laps around the track before you hit the showers!" (There was a big running track circling the field.)

The young guys started to run, but Satch was already on his way to the clubhouse. They were all yelling back at him, teasing, "Come on, Satch, two laps around the track." He stopped, waved at them, and explained his position. "I *throws* the ball to the plate, I don't *run* the ball to the plate."

Oddly enough, my father, who didn't know much about sports—though he did hold the football for me when I kicked off—was responsible for my encounter with one of the greatest athletes in American history. During the Depression, Bernie got a job with the WPA. He was a night watchman in Van Cortlandt Park, up in the Bronx, where they were doing some construction near the lake. I don't know what he was guarding, there was a bulldozer there, but who's going to come steal a bulldozer?

He stayed in a little shack with a potbellied stove and a cot, and he told me that every morning before the sun came up he'd look out and see a black man in sweats running as fast as the wind around the lake. He said the man always had a towel across his shoulders, and I decided he must be a fighter.

"If you behave this week," my father said, "on Friday night, I'll take you to work with me. You can sleep on the cot, I'll wake you up early, and you can see what I'm talking about."

That Friday night, I slept in the shack in the Bronx, while my old man stood watch, and at five-thirty Saturday morning, he woke me. It was a cool morning, and we stood outside watching this guy run, and I walked down closer to him, and he saw me. He stopped, asked me my name, and told me his.

I must have been about ten years old that day I met Jesse Owens, arguably the most amazing track and field star this country ever produced. In college, he'd broken world records for the 220-yard dash, the 220-yard low hurdles, and the running broad jump. At the 1936 Olympics, he'd won four gold medals, causing Hitler to walk out of the stadium rather than acknowledge that a black man could leave representatives of the master race in the dust behind him.

Owens was very handsome, very gentle, and I was awed by him.

At that point in my life, I'd never seen a great athlete. Up close, I mean. Years later, I was seated next to him at a dinner in Chicago, and I told him the story, and I started to choke up. (By now you've probably noticed, I choke easy.)

You take those early memories with you. All of us—even kings and queens and presidents—are in awe of people who excel. Because we live our dreams through them.

From my parents' apartment, it was only a short trolley car ride to Ebbets Field, which I thought of as Valhalla. WHN Radio broadcast a program featuring Happy Felton's Knothole Gang, and a kid could send in a box top from some product or other and become a Knothole Gang member. You got a card that admitted you to the ballpark for almost nothing, and you could sit in the bleachers and cheer the home team till you were hoarse.

I grew up with the fabled Brooklyn Dodgers—in the thirties, there was Lefty O'Doul; in the forties, there were Dixie Walker, Dolph Camilli, Pete Reiser, Jackie Robinson, Don Newcombe; in the fifties, Roy Campanella, Duke Snider, Carl Furillo—and I was a Dodgers nut.

The fans were as memorable as the team. A ragtag group of guys who called themselves the Brooklyn Dodgers Sym-phoney used to come to the ballpark with trumpets and bells, and there was also Hilda, crazy Hilda Chester, who ran all over the place banging a cowbell. She was the Apple Annie of baseball.

There was a Dodgers farm team—the Royals—in Montreal, and when I was older, working at the Tick Tock Club there, I always went to watch them play. Especially Jackie Robinson. I saw his last game before he left for Brooklyn to become the first black player in the majors.

At that time, New York was rich in major league baseball teams; we had the Yankees, the Giants, and the Dodgers. It was no fun to root for the Yankees; they never lost. The Dodgers, on the other hand, were always in last place, and any time they played the Giants at Ebbets Field, there were fistfights. If some idiot dared to root for the Giants, he was almost beaten to death with the rolled-up newspapers of Dodgers fans.

Sometimes, when I was still small, Jack Pollack, my sister Anita's husband, would take me to a game. He was a bettor, he bet baseball, and he wasn't the only one in the neighborhood who did. There was a guy known as Red Brown—a bookmaker who wore a white Borsalino hat—and one of my favorite baseball stories concerns him.

The World Series always took place at the same time as the Jewish high holy days, and I sang in synagogue, in my grandfather's choir. Since we kids were impatient to know how the Series was going, from time to time, one of us used to run outside, find a radio, listen for a few minutes, then come back and whisper the scores to the cantor, who would work them into his prayers.

He'd be chanting, and in the middle of the Yom Kippur service, you'd make out the words "Brooklyn two, Yankees four, in the bottom of the fifth." My grandfather knew what was going on, but he never said a word about it.

During the holidays, certain members of the congregation, usually those who had made large donations to the synagogue, would be called up to the altar where the rabbi would pay them special honor. The shammes, or custodian, would have notified them by postcard: "On such and such a day, you will be honored."

It happened this one year that Red Brown had got such a postcard, but it was World Series time, and he was at his busiest. Not only was he busy, he had to go to New Jersey to conduct his affairs, because Mayor La Guardia had recently chased all the bookmakers out of New York.

Still, he couldn't refuse the glory being offered him, so he was standing in the back of the synagogue, twitching. "When am I gonna get up there?" he asks the shammes. "I gotta get to my office in Jersey to take the bets." (It was serious business; there were twenty phones in some of those bookmaking establishments.)

"There's a lot of people here," says the shammes. "What are you pushing, what are you rushing?"

Red Brown fixes the shammes with a steely eye. "You know, every year, I give a hundred dollars to the synagogue." (That was a lot of money in the days when most people gave a dollar.) "If you can get me up to the rabbi early, I'll add another fifty."

So while the service is going on, and the cantor is singing, and my grandfather is sitting to one side, and all the kids in the choir, including me and my cousin Itchy, are restlessly shifting our feet, I see the shammes talking into my grandfather's ear. And my grandfather's face lights up. Next thing we know, he's calling Red Brown to the altar. The way it goes, the person being honored is brought before the rabbi, the rabbi reads a prayer, and into that prayer he inserts the name of the honoree.

Now since everybody in the congregation has not only an English name but also a Hebrew name, my grandfather leans toward Red Brown, and in Yiddish, asks his Hebrew name. "How do they call you?" And Red Brown says, "Cliffside four-seven-seven-eight-one." He gives his phone number. You never have seen such pandemonium in a synagogue, people are rolling on the floor.

But let me get back to that other bettor, Jack, my brother-in-law. When I started working at Leon and Eddie's, and hanging out at Toots Shor's, I met all the ballplayers. Especially the out-of-town players. If, for instance, the Cardinals were in New York, I might spot Stan Musial at the bar at Toots Shor's and say to him, "Come see the show at Leon and Eddie's."

My brother-in-law, convinced that I was in a position to pass him valuable inside information, information that would make him rich, approached me. "You're always around the sportswriters, you're always around the players, keep your ears open. You hear anything, let me know."

Shortly thereafter, on a Sunday, I was in Leon and Eddie's at the bar. Celebrity Night was in full swing, and a guy walked in bombed out of his head. I recognized Kirby Higbe, a pitcher who had been traded by the Dodgers to the Pittsburgh Pirates. And the Pirates were going to play the Dodgers on Monday. The very next day.

I phoned Jack and woke him up. "What is it?" he asked, none too warmly. "Jack," I said, "Kirby Higbe is in the bar at Leon and Eddie's, it's four o'clock in the morning, he's drunk, and I read in the papers he's probably the starting pitcher for the Pirates tomorrow."

Jack couldn't go back to sleep, he was so excited. He called Red Brown. "Fifty on the Dodgers," he said, "only if Kirby Higbe pitches for the Pirates." (When you bet a ball game, you can bet a certain pitcher. Meaning if that pitcher doesn't start, it's no bet.)

I got home about 9 A.M.—I was still living with my parents on Bedford Avenue in Brooklyn—and Jack was already there. "Come on," he said, "we're going to the ballpark, we gotta see this."

Sure enough, when we arrived at Ebbets Field, Kirby Higbe was warming up in the bull pen. He looked like he'd been hit by a truck. "This," said my brother-in-law, "is the biggest day of my life."

When they announced the starting pitcher was Kirby Higbe, Jack beamed. "You got a piece of the bet," he said, "for the information, you know."

Top of the first inning, the Pirates were up. They got no runs, no hits. Bottom half of the first inning, the Dodgers came to bat. Before Higbe was taken out, he gave up nine hits and five runs. And that was only the first inning. Jack's beam expanded.

Mistakenly, as it turned out. The Dodgers lost in the twelfth inning, 13 to 12. "You and your goddamn information," my brother-in-law was screaming.

"You got five runs," I said. "What more did you need?"

Now I was persona non grata with him. "Don't call me ever again," he said bitterly. Even when I was working at the Taproom, and the fighters and mob guys and bookmakers were coming in, he didn't want to know about it. Till the day he died, he never forgot Kirby Higbe—who ended up as a street corner preacher in Pittsburgh.

The Brooklyn Dodgers brought me pleasure, and they brought me pain. In 1954, with Leo Durocher managing, they actually won the pennant. In 1958, with Durocher managing the Giants, the *Giants* won the pennant. It was a terrible story. At the end of the 1958 season, the Dodgers and the Giants had been in a dead heat for first place, so a play-off game had been necessary.

And the play-off game led to the most famous moment in baseball. It happened at the Polo Grounds, which I had left sometime earlier. I'd been too keyed up to stay in the ballpark past the third inning. "Guys, I gotta go," I told my friends. "I can't stand the pressure."

I kept the radio on as I drove downtown to the 48th Street office I shared with Harry Adler, and when I got there, I went in and sat at my desk—it was an old desk I'd bought in a secondhand store, and it had a plate glass top, maybe a quarter inch thick—and watched the end of the game on television.

Don Newcombe was on the mound for the Dodgers, Bobby Thomson came up to the plate for the Giants, and Chuck Dressen, coaching third base, looked to the bull pen to bring in a relief pitcher. He called for Ralph Branca, Branca threw one pitch, Thomson hit the home run that came to be called the shot heard around the world, and I brought my hand down on my desk and split the glass top. I've still got the scar.

Whenever I present Ralph Branca to an audience, which happens a couple of times a year at some golf tournament, he walks over to me and says, "If you tell that goddamn Bobby Thomson story one more time, I'll break your arms." So I always say, "Ladies and gentlemen, I promise I'm not going to tell the story about Bobby Thomson hitting the home run," and I introduce Ralph Branca. He was a great pitcher who won a lot of ball games for the Dodgers, but he'll always be remembered as the guy who threw that pitch to Bobby Thomson.

Four years later, the Dodgers went to L.A., and I stopped watching baseball. There were all these New Yorkers trying to keep the team here, but Walter O'Malley, the owner, had sold us out, he'd already made the deal to move to Chavez Ravine. I realized then that I wasn't a baseball fan, I was a Brooklyn Dodgers fan.

At that juncture, I was a grown man who had been renting his own box in Ebbets Field. After the Dodgers skipped town, parts of the field—a piece of home plate, second base—were auctioned off, and a friend of mine bought me a souvenir, the eight seats from my box. They're still in my attic.

Although I myself was no Branca or DiMaggio, I'd always been involved in some kind of competitive sport, starting with my aborted boxing career, and after Jeanette and I moved to our little apartment in Long Beach, I took up golf.

We had one car, so Jeanette would drive me to the public golf course in the morning, and she'd go home—we had one baby then—and I'd play. I got very good, good enough to hustle and make money at it. And traveling around to work all over the country, I hooked up with other enthusiasts. Billy Eckstine was a rabid golfer; if we were on the same bill, we'd go out at six o'clock in the morning and play until we had to get back for our first show.

I got to know most of the legendary golfers of the day—Jimmy

Demaret, Cary Middlecoff, Sam Snead. Demaret changed the game, not because he was a great player—though he was—but because of the way he dressed. He wore red pants, gold pants, he was famous for his outfits. All those checked trousers and wild shirts you see now? He started it.

He became the pro at the Concord Hotel in the Catskills, and at the opening of the Concord's first golf course—it was still being constructed, but there were fairways and greens and tees—he and I played against Sammy Snead and Billy Eckstine. A big crowd turned out for the event. Trying to top Jimmy sartorially, I appeared in white pants, green-and-white shirt, black-and-white shoes, looking, I thought, every inch the dude. Demaret was, as always, loudly attired, and Sammy was wearing his straw hat, but Billy, a famously sharp dresser, outdid the rest of us.

On the first hole, my ball went off the fairway into the rough, an oozy quagmire. I went after it, took a swing, and was covered in mud to my eyebrows, I looked like Jolson doing "Mammy." I thought Demaret would have a heart attack laughing.

Unfortunately, as a golfer I had no sense of humor, and a terrible temper; I used to throw clubs, I used to break clubs. Once in Boston, while I was working for Lou Walters at the Latin Quarter, I was invited to play in a little tournament with a local hero named Teddy Bishop, who was then United States amateur champion. I'd been up all night, I had a big hangover, and I wasn't playing well anyway, because as my business got better, my golf got worse. I didn't have enough time to devote to it, and I was gambling at it, and all the guys I'd robbed over the years were now pouncing on me, killing me.

So this day in Boston, we teed off about 8:30 A.M. I had a caddy who looked like James Barton, stank of whiskey, and had a comic book rolled up in his back pocket.

I knew I was in for a bad time. And the worse I played, the more this guy annoyed me. Every time I'd ask, "Do you think it's a six iron or a five iron?" he'd just shake his head.

When I came up to a par three hole with a little Chinese bridge over a lake, I took a seven iron in my hand. I was about to address the ball, and the old drunk spoke. "Six iron," he said. They were the first words he'd uttered in twelve holes; he hadn't told me about a break on a green, hadn't told me anything, the poor bastard had just been dragging along, schlepping my clubs in a big heavy bag.

I backed away from the ball. "What did you say?"

"Six iron," he repeated, meaning the seven iron was not enough club. Now I was going to use a seven iron, no matter what. I hit the ball into the water. If you hit a ball into the water, there was a place where you could lay up, go down, and hit another shot. I got down there, took a wedge, and my caddy said, "Eight iron." I hit the wedge into the water. I was out. I walked back over the bridge, bumped into the old souse with the bag, and knocked him into the lake.

Next day, it was in the Boston papers. ALAN KING THROWS CLUBS AND CADDY INTO WATER. I didn't throw him into the water, I just bumped him, and he went right over the bridge.

Recently I played in a foursome with a guy who reminded me of myself forty years ago. Temper, screaming, throwing clubs. And I thought, What an idiot I was, it's only a game. But this guy didn't see it that way. He came to a water hole, hit four balls in a row into the water, walked up to the edge of the lake, took his golf bag, threw it into the lake, and marched off the course.

About two minutes later, the same guy came tearing down the hill, and jumped into the lake. We thought he'd gone berserk. But what had happened was, he'd had the keys to his car in his golf bag. He dredged up the bag, took out the car keys, threw the bag back into the lake, climbed up the hill again, and drove away.

I understood what he was going through; in the old days, I simply didn't have the temperament for the game. I was a basket case, I'd get up in the middle of the night to practice my swing. But I kept on playing. The year the Fontainebleu opened in Miami, Tony Martin and I were appearing there, and Jimmy Demaret showed up. He was in town to play in the Miami Open, and there were still a few slots available for amateurs and professionals who hadn't been in the draw. Jimmy suggested that I try to qualify. "What have you got to lose?"

I qualified—with the best two rounds of golf I ever played—and was elated; I was going to be in a major tournament. And even though part of it would take place on the golf course of a country club that didn't allow Jews, I couldn't be barred, because the tournament was a

PGA event. "If nothing else," Jimmy said, "you'll go where no Jew has ever gone before."

The first day, I went out and shot ninety-one. Ninety-one's the worst, hackers shoot better. I was going to kill myself; nobody dared talk to me. I couldn't hit a lick, and when I finished the round, I left the course, threw my bags in the car, and drove back to the Fontainebleu still wearing my golf shoes.

At the hotel, I got out of the car, and the parking valet heard the bang bang bang of my spikes on the cement driveway. "Mr. King," he said, "you still got your golf shoes on."

"Are you a golfer?" I said.

"Yeah," he said.

"What size shoes do you wear?"

"Nine."

Right there in the driveway, I took off the shoes and gave them to him. He looked at me, this lunatic standing in stocking feet. I opened the trunk, and by now, the doorman had come over. "Boy," he said, "that's some set of clubs."

"Do you play golf?" I said.

He said he did, and I handed him the clubs, and I never played golf again for thirty-five years.

Instead, I took up tennis. It was inevitable, because we'd moved to Great Neck, where everybody plays tennis.

I went to matches, and started to get friendly with the tennis crowd. It was easy, because by then I was a little bit of a celebrity, people knew me from the Sullivan show. One day I was at the bar of the old West Side Tennis Club in Forest Hills, and there was a guy standing beside me who looked like a movie star, with a face chiseled out of stone, and sun-bleached hair. He recognized me from TV, introduced himself as Lew Hoad, and said, in an Australian accent as thick as his arms, "Have a brew, mate."

Lew was one of the best tennis players who ever lived, and knowing him made my interest in the game twice as keen because now I was actually pulling for somebody.

He and his wife, Jennie, always stayed with us when they came to New York, and through them we met the other great Aussie players,

Rod Laver, Fred Stolle, Kenny Rosewall, Tony Roche, John New-combe, Roy Emerson.

Tony Roche and John Newcombe were just kids, and our guest house was like a tennis kibbutz. My wife, who's the neatest person in the world, used to go crazy, because there were socks and jockstraps all over the place.

By this time I'd built a tennis court, so the guys who came there could practice, and I'd sit and watch them. Sometimes I'd even hit with them, and I'd think, Here I am, a kid who played stickball in Brooklyn, and I'm practicing with Rod Laver, being coached by Lew Hoad, getting tips from Emerson and Stolle and Newcombe and Roche.

It didn't help; I was never very good, but I loved that world. After a while, I knew every tennis star I'd ever seen or read about. Arthur Ashe became my friend. I have a picture he sent me. On it he wrote, "If you had a backhand as big as your mouth, you'd be at Wimbledon."

I used to emcee sports dinners—still do—and I loved to work these guys over; I knew all their idiosyncrasies and crazy habits. I also officiated at a good many benefits, and finally, a grateful Billy Talbert—he was running the U.S. Open—asked, "What can *I* do for *you?*"

"I want a front box," I said. All the time the Open had been at Forest Hills, I'd been sitting up in the second or third tier. I didn't get along with the people who ran Forest Hills anyway; to me, they all looked like Rudy Vallee.

So Billy Talbert carved me out a box. Literally. He took seats from other boxes—you could see where the railings had been moved—and created Box 52 A, which I've had ever since, even after the Open moved to Flushing Meadows.

I don't think I ever enjoyed myself more than when I was around those tennis guys. I knew Vitas Gerulaitis when he was fifteen, and Bjorn Borg when he was sixteen. Partnered with John Newcombe, I played doubles in celebrity tournaments. We never won, but we had a good time.

One year, we were scheduled to play in the Robert F. Kennedy Celebrity Tournament—this was an event that started after Bobby died—but Newcombe, who had been skiing in Stowe, Vermont, had broken his leg.

I went to Tony Roche, who may have been the best left-handed doubles player in the world, and asked him to be my partner. "Tony," I said, "I've never won one of these things, and I want to. I want it more than anything, more than an Oscar."

"Okay," said Tony. "Just stand in the alley, and don't worry about a thing."

He and I went through the field. We started at nine o'clock in the morning, and by six o'clock that evening, we were in the finals against Rafer Johnson (who was the decathlon champion), and a top French player.

"Just stay at the net and hold on to that racket with both hands," Tony said, "because the Frenchman is going to slam the ball back at you."

Standing at the net, I shook. In the center court at Forest Hills! In the finals and the play-offs! Sudden death!

And we won. The ball was still in the air, and I knew it was out before they called it. I jumped over the net like I was the victor.

I have the film of it. Howard Cosell, covering the tournament for ABC, had interviewed me, saying, in his inimitable style, "Alan, you played in so many tournaments, how come you never won one before?"

And Tony Roche, in a voice just loud enough to be picked up by the mikes, had chimed in, " 'E never 'ad a partner before."

Afterward, I gathered a gang of about twenty-five friends, we went back to my house, and I opened champagne, and we started drinking out of this big bowl Tony and I had just won. In the midst of our drunken celebration, the phone rang. I picked it up and heard the voice of John Newcombe (who'd watched the match on television from his hospital bed in Vermont). "He never had a partner before!" Newcombe roared. "Put that son of a bitch on!"

When you win awards in your own business, it's nice, but to win this trophy when I wasn't even a good tennis player, that was something else. It sits on a shelf behind my bar now, and I never look at it that I'm not tickled. When I try to play the tape of that match for guests, somebody always says, "Oh, here he goes again," but I play it anyway. "Here," I say, "let me show you how I won Forest Hills."

I remember when Jimmy Connors, the hot new kid, was going to play Newcombe in a match. Looking for the fix, to give Newcombe a little edge, I went to Roy Emerson, who had a right hand like a vise. "Do me a favor," I said. "Before Jimmy goes out there, shake hands with him to wish him luck." I knew a handshake from Roy could crush Jimmy's fingers. After the handshake—I swear, it brought tears to Connors's eyes—Emerson walked back to me.

"You did it!" I said.

He just lifted his eyes to heaven. "Ass!" he said. "He's left-handed."

Newcombe beat Connors in a very tight match, without any help from me.

Connors was also involved in the most expensive finals—expensive for me, I mean—that I ever sat through. He'd destroyed Kenny Rosewall at Wimbledon, and now he was going to play him again at the U.S. Open. The match was set for a Sunday, but on Sunday it rained, so there was a postponement till Monday. I had to appear in Toledo, Ohio, for a big charity concert that Monday night, but I wasn't about to miss the finals.

I didn't know what to do. The match was going to start at two, best of five sets; it would probably go until five, six o'clock, so how could I get to Toledo on time? I solved the problem by calling up and renting a jet. It was going to cost ten thousand dollars to take me from La Guardia to Toledo, but La Guardia was only a few minutes away from Forest Hills. I knew no matter how long the match ran, when it ended, I had a plane waiting, and even if I had to change my clothes in midair, I wouldn't be late for the concert.

At two o'clock, Jimmy Connors took the court, and went on to beat Kenny Rosewall worse than he had beaten him at Wimbledon. It was all over by about ten minutes of three. I could have *walked* to Toledo, and not been late.

Speaking of Wimbledon, I stopped going there years ago, when I found myself spending an entire day in the back of a car in bumper-to-bumper traffic, only to get to the stadium and find the matches rained out, but in the days when I was still making the trek, I had some delicious experiences. One of them involved a doubles match that pitted Tom Okker and an Englishman named Mark Cox against Roy Emerson and Fred Stolle.

Now, do me a favor. Read the following paragraph out loud.

Emerson and Stolle served, and the first point was won by the other side. "Love–fifteen, Cox-Okker," said the referee. Emerson and Stolle lost the next point too. "Love–thirty, Cox-Okker," said the referee. By now, the staid British audience—including members of the royal family—had started to react to the referee's words. The referee, oblivious to what was happening all around him, said "Cox-Okker" about fourteen more times, until finally, right in the middle of the match, Roy Emerson ran over to him. "For God's sake," said Emerson, "call them Okker-Cox."

By then the stands were in an uproar, which was memorable; you don't often see hysterical spectators at Wimbledon.

Another Wimbledon high point. This time, I wasn't there, I was watching the matches over the BBC. Virginia Wade, a fine tennis player, had a peculiar stance. She used to hunker down, legs wide open, can out, and on the occasion I'm talking about, the very British announcer addressed himself to this idiosyncrasy. "Take note," he directed his listeners, "of the way Miss Wade stands there, her legs spread apart, crouching deeply, with her backside sticking out waiting to receive service."

In New York, whether at Forest Hills or in Flushing, fans have tended to be more unruly than fans at Wimbledon. So, for that matter, have the players. I've sat with Lew Hoad and watched Nastase or Connors or McEnroe carry on, and Lew, like Gary Cooper, would murmur without even moving his lips, "He'd never have pulled that with me."

This was probably true. Once Lew had walked into the locker room where an opponent who'd been disruptive was sitting, and he—Lew—had broken a metal locker with his fist, as if to say, "That could have been your head."

"Any time he played me after that," Lew said amiably, "he behaved properly."

Lew died in Spain, where he and Jennie went to live when they retired. The other Australians said he had been the greatest player of them all, and a good many non-Australians agreed with them.

Once, when I was doing an article for a tennis magazine about the top ten players in the history of the game, I interviewed Pancho Gonzales, the gifted Mexican-American star whose ego was as big as his serve. I didn't ask him who was the best he'd ever seen; he would have said "*I* was!" and he might well have been right. Instead, I said, "Pancho, what's the greatest match you ever played?"

Without pausing to think, he answered, "I beat Lew Hoad in a professional match, sixteen to fourteen in the fifth set." (As pros, Pancho and Lew had toured the world together.)

"What was the *second* greatest match you ever played?" I asked. "In Algiers," he said, "Hoad beat me in the fifth set, twelve to ten."

I gave up playing tennis when my legs quit; the game wasn't worth the pain (though if they'd let me play tennis with a golf cart, I'd still be out there on the court), and I went back to golf, which I'd abandoned thirty-five years earlier.

Harry Labe, my old fight manager from Montreal, had been with me in Florida when I gave away my clubs and my shoes. "Why are you carrying on like a maniac?" he'd said at the time, and I'd said, "Harry, I'll never play golf again. Ever."

He hadn't been impressed. "You're talking like an idiot. I'll bet you five hundred dollars you'll be back playing golf." I'd shrugged. "You got a bet."

Three years ago, I joined a country club on Long Island and started to play golf again. Now I was enjoying it for different reasons; I didn't give a damn anymore, I wasn't looking to win any bets or titles. And I was sitting in my office in New York, thinking about Harry Labe, who was by now in a home for the aged in Florida, and not doing very well, and I asked my secretary to bring me my checkbook. I made out a check for five hundred dollars and sent it to Harry.

A few days later, Harry telephoned. "Who the hell do you think you are?" he said. "I need five hundred dollars from you like I need another ache in my legs. I don't want your goddamn charity."

"Harry," I said, "it isn't charity. I'm back playing golf."

· · ·

When it comes to sports, I've been an amateur in the French sense of the word—a lover. And lucky in love, at that. Hacker or not, I've been privileged to spend time with phenomenal athletes, some of whom were also phenomenal human beings.

A few high points:

I played golf with Babe Didrikson Zaharias at Grossinger's (where she was the touring pro), and she was the best single athlete, male or female, I ever came across. She refused to play from the ladies' tee. She didn't need to, she could hit as far as anybody.

I emceed a party celebrating the hundredth anniversary of base-ball, and spent the evening just sitting and talking to Jackie Robinson, who'd had a profound impact on my life.

I substituted for Bob Hope—he was having an eye problem—at the College Football Hall of Fame dinner where Byron "Whizzer" White (the Supreme Court justice and former football star) was being honored, and during the reception, Sid Luckman, one of my earliest football idols, came up and asked me for an autograph for his grand-son. "You don't know who I am," he began, and I stopped him. "I not only know who you are, I had your picture over my bed in Brooklyn."

I got to know Joe Louis in Las Vegas, when he was working as a host in the casino at Caesar's Palace. He'd quiz me on prizefights. "Who beat so-and-so in such-and-such a year?"

When he was broke and dying in a hospital in Houston, Texas, Ben Rogers, a generous friend, took care of his bills. Worried that Joe didn't have many visitors anymore, Ben contacted me. "If I sent my plane for you," he said, "would you fly down and see him?"

I flew to Houston, went to the hospital—it was a Saturday after-noon—and found Joe sitting in a chair alongside his bed. The televi-sion set was on, and Sugar Ray Leonard was fighting. Sugar Ray's career was just beginning, Joe's life was winding down, and I sat in that room with the broken man who had been the greatest gentleman fighter anyone ever saw, and for an hour, we watched Sugar Ray.

The sports heroes of my past live in my head. If I close my eyes, I can still see Jesse Owens running around the lake in Van Cortlandt Park in the cool gray light of morning.

17 ✍ THE FRIARS

We few, we happy few,
we band of brothers.

—WILLIAM SHAKESPEARE

FOR HALF A CENTURY, I have been a member of the Friars Club. I'm now monitor of the Friars; I guess that means I get to clean the erasers. All of the long associations and friendships I've had in show business came out of the Friars Club, and it was Milton Berle who brought me in. The first time he saw me at Leon and Eddie's, I was doing an impression of him. When I came offstage, he gave me a cigar. "You gotta smoke a cigar," he said, "all comedians smoke cigars."

I began using a cigar as a prop, but I didn't smoke it, until Milton chided me again. "If you're gonna be a comedian, you gotta smoke cigars." So I started smoking cigars in my act; I didn't stop until four years ago, after they took out half my jaw.

In the joints where I worked, I became known as Milton Berle's protégé. Newspaper ads would read, in big letters, MILTON BERLE'S PROTEGE, and then in much smaller letters, ALAN KING.

I was seventeen years old when Milton introduced me to the wonders of the Friars. Young members were referred to as Friarlings, and I think we could join the club for twenty-five dollars.

Do you know what it was to be seventeen years old and walk into the clubhouse, the monastery? There, sound asleep in a big chair that looked like King Arthur's throne, was the great comedian Willie Howard. And there were Smith and Dale, Ted Lewis, Georgie Jessel, Al Jolson, every one a legend. To be part of all that seemed miraculous to me.

The club had been founded by George M. Cohan, Victor Herbert, and Will Rogers, mainly because of George M.'s affection for his father.

As a boy, George M. had been one of The Four Cohans, a vaudeville act that consisted of his parents, his sister Josie, and himself. The act closed with young George telling the audience, "My father thanks you, my mother thanks you, my sister thanks you, and I thank you." (Remember Cagney in the movie?)

George developed into a hugely successful actor, singer, dancer, writer. By the time he was twenty-six, in 1904, he had written the songs "Give My Regards to Broadway" and "I'm a Yankee Doodle Dandy," after which he turned out a dozen musicals and several straight plays, built a theater with his name on it, and became a big Broadway producer.

He and his father, Jerry Cohan, were both members of the Lambs (an actors' club that preceded the Friars), and Jerry was a first-team drinker. Retired from show business, time hung heavy on his hands, so he used to wait for the Lambs bar to open at 12 noon, and he'd hang out there all afternoon.

One day, he got into a drunken argument with the bartender, took his cane, and smashed every glass behind the bar. The House Committee brought him up on charges, and he was suspended for six months.

This poor old guy, they took his home away. He had no place to go. So George M. called a special meeting of the House Committee and begged the members to reinstate his father. Which they did.

Next day at noon, he was back at the Lambs, drinking in the bar, and a guy came over. "Mr. Cohan," he said, "we haven't seen you around the club for a while."

"I was on suspension," said Jerry.

"What did you do?" said the guy.

"This!" said Jerry, and he took his cane and broke all the glasses again, and he was thrown out of the Lambs for good.

What's a loyal son to do? Start the Friars, that's what, and give his old man a new place to go. I never knew George M. Cohan (he died in 1942) or Will Rogers or Victor Herbert, but I cherish that tale, as I cherish the club they established.

It was there I learned gin rummy because all the Friars played. Ted Lewis was the worst sore loser, and nothing gave me more pleasure than aggravating him. He was famous for the line "Is *everybody* happy?" so before I said "gin!" I would say, "Is *everybody* happy?" and everyone in the room would know I had gin, and Ted Lewis would go bananas.

Eventually, a delegation of Friars came to me. "You've got to stop torturing Ted Lewis. He's complaining so much he's making everybody crazy."

I said okay. A few days later, Ted and I were playing, and I looked at my hand, and I had gin. "Excuse me, Ted," I said, "I'll be right back."

"Where you goin' in the middle of the hand?" he said suspiciously.

"I gotta go to the john—"

"No, you finish the hand!"

"I don't care what you say, I'm going to the john."

I left the room, picked up a house phone, and asked the operator to page Ted Lewis. I could hear the phone ringing, and Ted picked up. "Is *everybody* happy?" I said into the mouthpiece. "Gin!"

I'm not even going to tell you how he carried on.

Lou Walters, a Friar who owned the Latin Quarter, was another of my gin opponents. Lou was very good to me (I worked for him many, many times), but he had one blind eye, and when we played gin, I'd toss the cards toward the bad eye, hoping he'd miss something. With the good eye, he'd glare at me. "You think I don't know what you're doing, you little bastard?"

Bob Hope was a Friar too. I was fond of Bob, but it was his wife, Dolores, that I loved. I would always flirt with her—she's the most beautiful, charming woman—and Bob thought the flirting was cute.

I remember once when their house in California burned down and he was grousing: "Dolores wants to redo the place; it would cost a fortune." (Bob is a prince, but a very frugal prince.)

By then, I knew the Hopes pretty well. "You ought to be ashamed of yourself," I said. "You've got all the money in the world, and here's this woman who's tolerated you for all this time, how can you not let her fix up her house?"

I literally embarrassed him. For years after that, every time we saw each other, I'd say, "Where's Dolores?" and he'd say, "You know where she is, she's in France with a pansy decorator spending my money, and it's all your fault."

A couple of years ago, when I did the television series *Inside the Comedy Mind,* I wanted to interview Bob. I called, and he wasn't feeling very well, but he couldn't have been more gracious, so I went out to the Hope place in Toluca Lake. Dolores and I conferred, both worried that Bob, who was born in 1903, might forget his own stories.

So what I did was, I had one camera on me, and one camera on Bob. When he had a little trouble, I would jog his memory—"You know, the time you met Dolores and George Murphy"—and he'd be off and running. Afterward, all I had to do was edit myself out of the tape.

One of the stories he told went back a long time. He had been doing two or three shows a day, working either the Palace or Loew's State—this was before he became a big star in musicals and radio and movies—and somebody came backstage and told him Charlie Chaplin was eating at Dinty Moore's restaurant. It was snowing, but Bob, all excited, mushed over to Dinty Moore's and stood outside, waiting for Chaplin to emerge. And when Chaplin came out, and was stepping into his limousine, Bob stopped him. "Mr. Chaplin," he said, "my name is Bob Hope, and I'm working in vaudeville, and I just want to shake your hand."

We were coming to the end of the interview—the tape was still running—and I said, "Bob, you told that story about Charlie Chaplin, now I'm going to tell you a story about Bob Hope. I was a starstruck kid, hanging around the Friars Club, and another Friarling told me Bob Hope was eating in Dinty Moore's. It was raining, I swear to God, it was raining, and I ran out of the club and went over to Dinty

Moore's and waited in the street until you came out. And then I stopped you and said, "Mr. Hope, I'm Alan King, a young comedian, and I just want to shake your hand."

Right on camera, Bob started crying; when I put the show together, I ended with that scene.

After our encounter outside of Dinty Moore's, Bob used to come and see me at Leon and Eddie's. He always treated me as an equal, never played the big man. A lot of the Friars were like that. I think they realized I worshiped them, and I knew more about them than they knew themselves. I read, and I listened, and I worshiped.

I have my own story about meeting Charlie Chaplin. It has absolutely nothing to do with the Friars, but I'm going to put it here anyhow.

Bob Hope was host of the Academy Awards ceremonies for almost thirty years, until 1969, when the choreographer and director Gower Champion was brought in to liven up the proceedings. Champion announced that it was "boring" to have a permanent emcee; in 1969, he wanted ten "Friends of Oscar" (including Frank Sinatra, Jane Fonda, and Ingrid Bergman) to share the chores. (*TV Guide* reported that when Champion telephoned Bob to tell him about the new format, Bob said, "Thank God.")

Three years later, the Academy was still toying with multiple hosts, so in 1972, I was one of four—Helen Hayes, Sammy Davis Jr., and Jack Lemmon were the others—to take on the job.

Charlie Chaplin, who hadn't been back to the United States for thirty years, was flying to New York to be honored by the Film Society of Lincoln Center, and in Hollywood, the Academy jumped on the bandwagon, inviting him to come west and take home his second Honorary Oscar.

He accepted the invitation, his return from exile made headlines, Candice Bergen shot his picture for the cover of *Life,* and on Academy Awards Night (because protesters were threatening demonstrations against him and his "left-wing leanings") he was spirited into the Dorothy Chandler Pavilion through an underground garage.

Helen Hayes was the first of us hosts to appear, and I was the second. I came out with a cigar and did a monologue. Neil Simon, a writer-producer named Bob Ellison, and I had worked it out together, and it was pretty good.

I brought Ellison and his wife to California with me—that was his payment for helping with the monologue—and he was waiting backstage with me. I was having my usual gin, and this made Ellison nervous. "Alan, this is the Academy Awards, stop drinking before the show."

"I always have a few drinks before a show," I said. "Would you go back and get me another gin?"

He brought me the drink, I took one gulp, realized it was water, and then I heard, "Ladies and gentlemen, Alan King."

I went out there, did nine really strong minutes, and walked off. Bob Ellison was in the wings jumping up and down with pleasure, and I went up to him and said, "Don't you *ever* give me water when I ask for gin."

He stared at me, his mouth open. "That's the only thing that's on your mind now?"

Actually, I had a lot of things on my mind, including Charlie Chaplin. I'd never met Chaplin, I hadn't even seen him yet. They'd built him a little greenroom with a TV monitor in it so he could sit and watch the proceedings, and the way the stage was built, there was a tunnel that led almost up to the microphone. This meant that when Chaplin came out of the tunnel, he didn't have far to walk.

At the beginning of the evening, the president of the Academy, Daniel Taradash, had told the audience it was only six days till Chaplin's eighty-third birthday, and said, "We welcome him home."

At the end of the evening, a montage of film clips from Chaplin's movies was shown, and as the last shot faded, Charlie Chaplin was revealed, standing alone onstage.

I don't have to tell you. They give standing ovations for everything out there, but this night, in this place, there was the most tremendous ovation I'd ever heard. From where I stood, I could see Chaplin coming out of the dark onto the stage, and before my eyes, when the light hit him, this little, almost invalid, old man turned into a giant.

Visibly moved by his reception, he said, "Words are so futile," and then Jack Lemmon brought out the cane and derby that had been

Chaplin's trademark when he was the most beloved clown on the planet, and Chaplin put the hat on, and the applause started all over again.

I still hadn't met him. He was well protected. And nobody knew if he would be too fragile to come to the Beverly Hilton for the Governor's Ball and the big dinner following the ceremonies.

Jeanette and I were already in the ballroom when we heard a commotion on the other side of the room. Everybody stood up and applauded, and here came Charlie Chaplin with his wife, Oona. They had set a table for him on the first balcony, and after about five minutes, when the noise had died down, a man tapped me on the shoulder. "Mr. King," he said, "Mr. Chaplin would like to say hello to you."

"Come on," I said, grabbing Jeanette. We were led to Chaplin's table, which was surrounded by security guards, and Chaplin reached out and took my hand. "That was a wonderful monologue," he said, and talked to me for two minutes. Then he kissed me on the back of one hand.

In a state of shock, I returned to my own table. I was thinking about a movie called *Gentleman Jim*. In the picture, John L. Sullivan (played by Ward Bond) is the world's heavyweight champion, an Irish god, and a very gregarious man. When he stops for a couple of beers, he shakes hands with everyone in the bar. So Alan Hale (as the father of Jim Corbett, played by Errol Flynn) comes home one night, and his family is sitting out on the stoop, and he has his hand stuck out like there's something wrong with it. Young Jim says, "What happened to your hand, Pop?" and Alan Hale, in a heavy brogue, says, "You're lookin' at the hand that shook the hand of the great John L. Sullivan."

Funny, the things that stay in your mind. I came back from meeting Chaplin and I had my hand stuck out that same way, and Arthur Krim, then head of United Artists, sitting at the next table, said, "What happened to your hand?" And I said, "Arthur, you're lookin' at the hand that shook the hand of the great Charlie Chaplin."

Now back to the Friars. Milton Berle saved the club. It had gone broke, and we'd had to give up our building. We moved into the Edison Hotel because a generous Friar named Nathan Kramer, who owned the place, gave us two rooms there, a sitting room and a card room.

Milton, the abbot of the Friars, had been a big star since the thirties. (Long before he became Uncle Miltie on television, he'd made $25,000 a week playing the Carnival Room of the Capitol Hotel, for a solid year.) Now he started having dinners, using his popularity to raise money to restore the club, and the program worked. Our beautiful building on East 55th Street is a far cry from the two rooms in the Edison where Milton started plotting to rescue us.

But for him, we'd have been out of business.

Over time, the Friars developed a Round Table to rival the Round Table at the Algonquin. At least, we thought so. When everybody moved to California, our Round Table was reborn at the Hillcrest Country Club, but East or West, it was the same guys sitting there—Lou Holtz, Groucho, George Burns, Jack Benny, Jessel—and it had the same ambience.

Joe E. Lewis followed Milton as abbot of the Friars, but the gravity of the honor didn't sober him up. When we were both staying at the Drake Hotel in Chicago—I was working the Chicago Theater, he was working the Chez Paree—he'd be so loaded I'd have to put him to bed every night. He'd just married a movie actress, a pretty girl named Martha Stewart, and she was in Miami doing a picture, and this one night he came home bombed, called her in Miami, and woke her up. Then he fell asleep on his end of the phone, she fell asleep on her end of the phone, and he got a phone bill for $270.

When she divorced Joe E., he was heartbroken. He was about to go into the Copa, and the Friars en masse decided to show up for the second show on his opening night. Everybody wanted to protect Joe, who was really torching, and had been drinking for days.

Even when he was working, he drank. He used to have a shot glass on every ringside table. The trumpet player would blow the racetrack's "Call to the Colors," and Joe E. would lift a glass, say, "It is now post time," and knock back the whiskey. So of course he'd get progressively drunker as the show wore on.

He used to throw in funny little phrases all through his act. He'd say something like, "You can lead a horse to water, but if you can get him to lie on his back and float, then you got something." Or: "Show me a friend in need, and I'll show you a pain in the ass." After each of these profound observations, he'd lift his glass—"It is now post time"—and wet his whistle.

One time, the trumpeter played the fanfare, Joe E. raised his glass, announced, "It is now post time," had a belt, then added, "La si cum yay, la soo cum yah." The audience looked bewildered. What the hell did he say? Joe E. shrugged. "I read it on a can of sardines. They wouldn't put it on a can of sardines if it didn't mean something."

Totally inane hilarious things he used to do. Then he'd forget what the next song was supposed to be, and Austin Mack, the piano player who'd been with him for, I don't know, fifty years, would have to play three notes to give him the melody and the cue. Joe always made jokes about Austin Mack. "I'd like you to meet my pianist, the late George Apley. He passed away three days ago, but nobody had the guts to tell him."

Now his wife is divorcing him, he's torching, he's at the Copa drunk, and we're all there to lend moral support. He goes through a couple of songs, a few jokes, but you can see he's running down, and you can feel the audience, which adores him, starting to get tense. Out of the blue, he begins a story:

"You know, a man can have many women in his life, but when you look back, there's always one special woman." He's going on with this sorrowful tale, and I'm sitting there with Jeanette and all the Friars, and I'm saying to myself, *God, Joe, God, Joe, get on with it, Joe.* And he's got the glass in his hand, and it seems like it's been an eternity.

The audience is panicked for him, Austin Mack is hitting the three notes for the next song, but Joe continues telling this torch story to the audience. I'm dying for him. "But you know," he says, "with that one woman, there's always one song," and his voice cracks, and there's a tear in his eye, and he turns to Austin Mack and says, "Roll Out the Barrel."

That was the biggest fucking laugh I ever heard in my life. First of all, it came from relief. Joe E. was a master showman. *"Roll Out the Barrel."* Now *that's* funny. It wasn't that he'd suckered us in, either. He was on his way to absolutely stripping himself naked out there, telling all, and then a light hit him.

I was so blessed to have watched him, to have watched the whole cast of characters who were the Friars. It was an incredible time, and though I don't know if I realized I was learning, I absorbed by osmosis the lessons they taught. Each one had his own trick, a nuance, a personal way of doing things. Some of those people were even bigger than the stories about them.

Though when I go into a restaurant with Milton, and he begins telling anyone who will listen, "I started him in this business, I gave him his first cigar," I wince. Last time it happened, I said, "Yeah, you also gave me cancer."

Today, there are a lot of wonderful young comedians who make me laugh, but the ones I like best have a sense of history and tradition. Richard Pryor, Billy Crystal, Robin Williams, they don't get into bed at night saying, "Today, I invented show business."

Of course, it's personal. To me, the greatest entertainer of all was Sammy Davis Jr. There simply was nothing he couldn't do. One night in Lake Tahoe, George Burns and I were sitting at a table watching him, and he was dancing, singing, offering impressions, playing the trumpet, he was all over the place. Besides talent, the man had the energy of a brewery horse. And George, who had been around forever, turned to me and said, "I never saw anything like it."

Wanting confirmation of my own good taste, I said, "Is he the greatest entertainer you ever saw?" George stopped, thought, then said, "Yes." Long pause. "Except for Al Jolson."

I used to ask people what it was that Jolson *had*. They'd just say he was indescribable. (Much later, I found out some of what he had when a young friend and historian named Bruce Charet gave me everything Jolson had ever done on film—seven and a half hours on cassette. I once sat at home in a rainstorm and played it all—musical numbers from the movies, radio shows with Bing Crosby and Oscar Levant, even his audition for *Jolson Sings Again*. He screen-tested for the part of Al Jolson, but didn't get it.)

It was after *The Jolson Story* came out, in 1946, that the Friars were planning to honor Sophie Tucker in the grand ballroom of the Waldorf, and I was on the planning committee, as assistant stage manager. Someone in the know told me Jolson might come. "But if he does come, he doesn't want to sit on the dais."

Jolson could be very difficult, but because of the movie, he was a big star again. Furthermore, he and Sophie Tucker were old pals, so we all hoped he would grace her party with his presence, but the only thing we kept hearing was, "I may come, I may not come."

The evening of Sophie's tribute arrived, everyone was seated, having dinner, speeches and show about to begin, when Jolson, star of stars, made his entrance in a black tuxedo, with a black turtleneck sweater and a suntan. He always had a suntan.

Jessel was the emcee, and he sent an emissary over to the great man, at his table. "We know you don't want to sit on the dais, but would you just do a song?"

No, says Jolson, "I just want to sit here."

There are a thousand people in the ballroom, by now they know Jolson's there, and they're craning their necks to see him. Still, the show progresses smoothly, and finally Jessel says, "Ladies and gentlemen, this is the easiest introduction I ever had to make. The world's greatest entertainer, Al Jolson."

The place is going wild. Jolson gets up, takes a bow, sits down. Could he milk an audience. I'm watching this from offstage. He doesn't sit down too fast, and as he sinks into his chair, the people start banging with their feet, and he gets up, takes another bow, sits down again.

It's chaos, and slowly, he seems to relent. He walks up onto the stage—not the dais, the stage—and says, "Sophie," and he starts talking about her, getting a few laughs, but the people are yelling, "Sing! Sing! Sing!" He milks that for another minute. Then he says, "I'd like to introduce you to my bride," and this lovely young thing gets up and takes a bow. The audience doesn't care about the bride, they don't even care about Sophie Tucker. "Sing! Sing! Sing!" they're screaming again.

"My wife has never seen me entertain," Jolson says, and looks over toward Lester Lanin, the orchestra leader. "Maestro, 'Is It True What They Say About Dixie?'"

He sang ten songs that night; they wouldn't let him get off the stage. (Legend has it that Enrico Caruso, at that time the world's greatest singer, who did many Sunday night benefits at the Winter Garden, set one rule: "I do not go on after Jolson.")

I know Jolson was great. Even though I didn't care about him, I know he was great. But better than Sammy Davis?

Not that other artists (other than Sammy, I mean) didn't affect me. I've never listened to Louis Armstrong without a big grin on my face. He was just so full of fun and life and music. Barbra Streisand is prodigious too. I first saw her at the Bon Soir, a nightclub in the Village. There was this girl with a big nose, dressed in a schmatta that Edith Piaf would have rejected, and she was up on the stage talking in a Brooklyn accent, and I thought she was a comedienne. All of a sudden, I heard this voice open up, and I fell back, stunned. Some comedienne.

I also loved the Ritz Brothers. The two older ones, Al and Jimmy, belonged to a club with my uncle Hymie, and they danced at my mother's wedding. Not Harry, he was too young. Harry was the little guy in the middle, who rolled his eyes, and I think he was the funniest man who ever lived. When the brothers were working in Miami, they'd stay in the penthouse of the Lord Tarlcton Hotel, and every morning, the three of them would get up, walk out onto their balcony, and moon the public. They'd stand there with their asses hanging over the edge, and everyone would say, "The guy in the middle is the funny one."

The Ritz Brothers were Friars too.

Incidentally, the Friars, who were so special when New York was the show business capital of the world, are making a big comeback. The young stars who moved to California have rediscovered the club, and when they're in New York, they all come in, so we're having a renaissance.

Every night at six o'clock, I hold court there. I stand at the bar, drinking my gin and telling stories like my predecessors, the guys who did it before me.

It's a joyful thing to look back. I was at Billy Crystal's anniversary party in Los Angeles, and a bunch of the young comics were standing around me while I was going on about the old days, when my wife came up and touched my arm. "Come on," she said, "it's enough already with these stories. You're turning into Jessel."

I looked at her. "Yes," I said. "Maybe I am."

It's tradition, and that's what the Friars is all about.

18 ✑ JEANETTE'S TURN

Because of Alan, I met the Queen of England, I saw Clark Gable up close.

FIRST OF ALL, we were kids together. I think that he proposed when I was ten, and he was eleven. We sat on the stoop of the house where my family lived, and he said, "Someday you're going to marry me."

I went upstairs and told my mother. She said, "Jeanette, go to sleep, you'll be fine."

My parents knew his parents and his grandfather; we all lived in a kind of ghetto in Williamsburg, and everybody knew everybody else's family. I was a very protected child, and content to be protected. I never really ventured further than that little area we lived in, I wasn't at all sophisticated, and I'm still not.

But we talked, Alan and I, and I knew. He was always with me, no matter what I did. My family would go to Rockaway Beach for the summer, and you could bet he'd show up in Rockaway Beach to check on how I was, and to spend the day.

We both went to junior high, but that's as much as he went to school. I continued on to high school, he didn't. He wasn't like any-body else in the neighborhood. He worked at night, he went off to New York, he told us stories about places he'd been and people he'd met, and everybody except me thought he was making it all up. And, as I said, he never put a foot in high school. How could my hard-working, foreign-born father not disapprove? "Why do you need this?" he asked me.

But my father had come to this country with nothing, and he was very busy making his fortune, which more or less left the ball in my mother's court. And my mother was smart. "If you love him," she said, "there's nothing we can do about it." I didn't know if I loved him; I didn't even know what love was. How could I? I had no frame of ref-erence, I only knew that he was there, very strong, very ambitious, all the things I wasn't.

He said he was going to make it one way or another, he was going to become successful, he was going to have all the things he'd ever wanted, he was never again going to wear his brother-in-law's hand-me-down jackets. And I believed him. I believed that was what he was going to do, I bet on him, and I have not been disappointed.

"If you love him, there's nothing we can do about it." She didn't go, "rah rah rah," my clever mother, none of that, but she didn't de-mand that I walk away from him, either.

If she had, I couldn't have married him. Back then, we didn't want to do anything that would make our parents uncomfortable or un-happy. Today, your child comes to you and says, "I'm moving in with this girl," "I want this," "I need that," and it doesn't matter what you think about it. It's "Deal with it, because that's what I'm going to do."

I never wanted to give my parents a moment's concern. I was the first of their children to leave the nest (my brother was older than I, my sister was younger), and I never shared with them any of the dif-ficult side of marriage to Alan; I never would tell them I was lonely, or frightened, or that I felt insecure.

I gave up the idea of college because Alan asked me to. He was in show business, he worked odd hours, and he wanted me to be there when he got home.

That may have been the framework of our early marriage. He

wanted me to be there, and I was. I was too shy to make my own moves. I've known a lot of people who would have picked themselves up and got a job, but at seventeen and eighteen, I couldn't have done it. I didn't have the self-esteem to demand my place and my space. That didn't come to me for a number of years, and then all of a sudden, I grew up. I'm not anything like that girl he started off with.

But back at the beginning, my fears fit right in with his needs. I never bucked my mother, I never bucked my father, and I certainly wasn't going to buck Alan. Whatever had to be would be.

It wasn't the best part of my life, it really wasn't. But I don't think a marriage of fifty years lasts unless the two people change. And I also think, looking back, that it's more of a credit to him than to me that our marriage survived. He came from such a poor family, and suddenly the world was there in front of him, he was exposed to every enticement he might have dreamed about when we were children. He could have packed up and said, "That's it, I'm gone," he could have found a girl who was more worldly than I, but he knew what was good for him, he always came home.

Alan's mother didn't love me, I could never make it there, but his father was different. His father was a lot like Alan. He was charming, he was bright, and bottom line, he was crazy about me. I adored him. How can you not love someone who's crazy about you? He'd call me when he wanted to put money in the bank (it was Alan's money anyway), and we went all over Brooklyn to little banks. He had three hundred dollars here, two hundred dollars there, he'd saved it all up, and he didn't trust anybody but me; he made me executor of his estate.

When he wanted to be sure he had burial space, he came to me again. "Jeanette, you're the only one who'll listen, I want you to take care of it." And I did. It wasn't hard to do, with my father in the business.

Alan bought a family plot, and we drove his father out to see it. It was in Mount Hebron, one of the oldest cemeteries on Long Island, right at the beginning of the Long Island Expressway. It was also near Shea Stadium and the Flushing Meadows tennis facility.

We were standing on a knoll, and Alan's father looked out over the landscape as though he were buying waterfront property. "What's that over there?" he said, waving one arm. "That's Shea Stadium, where the Mets play," Alan said. "And what's that building behind it?" "That's the Flushing Meadows Tennis Center," I told him, "where they hold the U.S. Open."

"Oh," said Bernie, and nodded. "Then I'm sure he'll come to visit my grave at least once a year."

Alan is a man of great imagination, he has wild fantasies, and his father was the same way. Even when he was very old, he could still fantasize a relationship with a woman he scarcely knew. One day I was sitting with him in the Hebrew Home for the Aged, and this lady came over and said fiercely, "Stay out of my room!" Would you believe it? The man was ninety years old, he could hardly move in his wheel-chair, yet he was running around at night. (I use the word *running* loosely.)

Early in our marriage, Alan and I had our sons, Bobby and Andy, and I had to make a choice. Much as I'd wanted children, I decided that my husband had to come first. I had to make time for Alan in or-der for our marriage to work.

I'd tend the children all day, and at 6 P.M., I would take a quick shower, get dressed and done up, say good-bye to the kids and the sit-ter, hop in the car, and be off to Manhattan to meet Alan. And I'd stay out as long as he wanted to stay out. We'd get home at three, four in the morning, and my kids were up at six, and I was up with them. I'm not saying anyone would have given me the award for Mother of the Year, but I was there, I made sure they were clean and fed, I did the best I could.

It wasn't always wonderful. Children need parents, they need un-derstanding, they don't take kindly to being shuffled around, but Alan was on the rise, he was going, and there was no question in my mind that I was going with him.

I believe Andy and Bobby might not have had some of the prob-lems they had if we'd been better parents, more mature parents, and if Alan had been around more. He was always traveling, working clubs and theaters, and he couldn't afford to take the family along. Besides, we didn't want to disrupt the kids' routine.

So when he was on the road, I stayed behind. I never went to England when he was working with Judy, and I didn't go to Vegas much, either. Even when he was performing in New York, I didn't get into the city every single night. But that didn't mean he came rushing home the minute he'd taken his bow. After work, he liked to stop off for a nightcap at Billy Reed's Little Club, where he always met somebody he knew. Once, he walked in and there were Joe E. Lewis and Frank Sinatra and a whole gang of friends, and he sat drinking with them until four o'clock in the morning and then explained he couldn't go home. "I'm gonna get killed."

They wrote him a note like you'd write to the teacher. "Dear Jeanette, just to tell you that Alan was with us, and we wouldn't let him go, it isn't his fault."

Another morning, he came home at 5 A.M., thinking he could sneak in, and found to his dismay that all the lights were on. The plumbing had broken, there was a riot in the house, and he was spotlighted creeping along the driveway like an unlucky burglar.

When he was out of town, I waited and worried. About everything, including women he might meet on the road. Worrying was all I could do, unless I wanted to blow the whole thing. Though I did make my position clear in, I am sorry to tell you, a rather crude way. "Don't you dare embarrass me," I said, "because if you ever embarrass me, I'll cut your balls off."

So he didn't embarrass me, but he did, on occasion, infuriate me. Once, he came home from England with a valet. This little guy shuffled into our tiny ranch house in Rockville Centre. We had two bedrooms, one bathroom, and a kind of sitting room where Alan installed the gentleman's gentleman.

I was timid, but there were limits, even for me. My outrageous husband had been in England, and on the spur of the moment, he decided that he was going to be a titled person. Here I had two boys who were a handful, three years apart, and wild—I can tell you I didn't know where to go first, what to hang on to first—and I'm getting ready to bathe them, and here came this man into the bathroom with a thermometer.

He wanted to run water in the tub and test the temperature.

"What are you doing?" I said. "Well," he said, "Mr. King is going to have a bath." I said, "Mr. King is going to have a bath, huh?"

I went and found Alan and took him into our bedroom. "This is a very nice man," I said, "and I feel very sorry for him, but you brought him all the way from England, so you'd better find somebody who needs him. You don't need him to run your bath. Take a shower."

He never did anything like that again. Though he did bring a Rolls-Royce (a Silver Cloud) all the way from England, too. That time, we were both excited about the import. The night it arrived, Alan parked it in front of the house—we lived in a cul-de-sac, with little houses all around, houses filled with friends and their babies, nobody in show business, just regular people—and we went around knocking on the neighbors' doors. All our friends came out, and we gave them rides.

We had the best times in that car, and in that house, but then everything got too small. Alan was doing all these television specials, we were getting television sets that were bigger than our rooms, and we had a $35,000 car parked in front of a $25,000 house. It was just all wrong.

Someone recommended a bigger house—the old Oscar Hammerstein mansion—in Great Neck, and we went to look at it. It was so grand I was stunned. "My God, Alan," I said, "this is impossible. We can't do this."

We stood there at the edge of the water—the house slopes down to Long Island Sound—and stared back at this castle, and Alan said, "I'm going to buy this house."

I was frightened. In those days, I was always frightened. "Alan, how are we going to pay for this house?"

"We're going to buy this house," he said again, and he phoned his manager, and his manager said, "You buy that house," so we bought it.

I don't think even the people who sold it to us believed we could do it, because we were two kids, but we worked it out, though at first we didn't have the money to really fix it. It's very big, and inside, it was all painted a funny color green, and my boys and my nephews used to come and play in it. They called it a ghost house, they thought it was weird. Finally we got it cleaned up, and—leave it to him—Alan got

Melanie Kahane, a very good, very expensive decorator, to do it over. We've been in it for thirty-five years.

I've said I stayed behind with the children when Alan was on the road, but never in the summers. Summers, the boys went to camp, and we went to Europe.

My boys hated camp. They used to mail me ransom notes. Bobby once sent a letter with the edges of the paper all charred. "The bunk's on fire," he wrote, "but that's okay." He and Andy behaved so badly the camp didn't want to keep them.

Even so, I went to the south of France, to Italy, to Israel, with my husband. I needed to feel a part of Alan, and he needed to show me he wanted me to be a part of him. Still, the boys felt abandoned.

When we had our daughter, Elainie, I got another shot at motherhood, and I did it differently. I did it better. First of all, I was older, and I had money. I also—at long last—thought I was entitled to take a stand. "There's no way we go anywhere without our daughter and the nurse," I told Alan. "We're all together. If you play Vegas, I'm there, the baby is there, the nurse is there."

Where we went, our daughter went. What we did, she did.

Despite our early mistakes—teenage parents make a lot of mistakes—our boys are doing fine, thank God, and so is Lainie, and we have adorable grandchildren, any one of whom can program a VCR. This convinces me they are all geniuses, since I can't touch one of those machines without screwing it up.

Because of Alan, I have been so lucky. I've met the Queen of England, and I saw Clark Gable up close. It was wonderful.

The Gable viewing took place in one of the years when Alan was working with Tony Martin. Tony gave him two tickets to the Academy Awards, so Alan brought me to California. I was thrilled. Here I was, a little girl from Williamsburg, Brooklyn, Izzy and Bella's daughter, and I kept saying to myself, Imagine, you're going to the Academy Awards!

I got all dressed up, and Alan got all dressed up, but we didn't realize we were really like two shnooks, nobody knew us, nobody had invited us to any of the post-Oscar parties, we simply had two tickets to go to the Academy Awards. We were like dress extras.

We attended the Awards, we watched Fred Astaire walk in—he didn't really walk, he danced in—and I was in heaven. After the ceremonies, we left the theater, and we didn't know what to do.

"Let's go to Romanoff's," Alan said.

We had the driver of our rented limousine take us to Romanoff's. It was the most chic restaurant in Hollywood, owned by Prince Mike Romanoff. He was a prince like Alan was a king.

"You sit in the car," Alan instructed me, "and I'll go in and see if anybody's there."

He went in, he came out. "Okay, let's have a drink."

"Who's in there?" I said.

"Never mind," he said, "let's go."

We sashayed into the restaurant, and there was Clark Gable standing at the bar, bigger than life. He *was* bigger than life—his face was bigger than most faces, his shoulders were bigger than most shoulders, he was a big, big, big man. I kept whispering, "That's Clark Gable, that's Clark Gable, that's Clark Gable—"

Clark Gable certainly didn't know who we were, but we were wearing evening clothes, so it was easy to figure out where we'd been. And since we were only a couple of feet away from him, and he was a very nice man, he spoke to us. "What did you think of the Awards?"

"I thought Judy Garland should have won," said my husband, the seasoned Academy Awards expert. (Alan hadn't yet met Judy, but that was the year she was nominated for *A Star Is Born*, and lost to Grace Kelly in *The Country Girl*.)

"I was rooting for Judy too," said Gable. "You didn't go to any of the parties?"

"Well," said Alan, "I don't like being in those big crowds," and Clark Gable said, "I feel the same way."

That's typical of what happens when you're out with Alan. The restaurant was empty, nobody had arrived yet, they were all at parties, but Clark Gable was there, and to this day, I don't know why. I only know he was there and I saw him.

Now, some forty years later, I can tell you I've been to a lot of fancy parties and met a lot of famous people, but my favorite famous person has always been Frank Sinatra.

Sinatra was someone I loved as a teenager, and all of a sudden, he was my friend. I've stayed in his house. He carried me into the Kennedy inaugural gala because he didn't want my shoes to get wet. He came to Andy's bar mitzvah in a yacht with orange trim—he likes orange, he thinks it's cheerful—and I took Lainie, who was then three years old, down to the dock to meet him. She had big blue eyes and long blond hair, and he took one look, and melted. "My God," he said, "it's a wonderful little child." It was as though he didn't quite believe that anything so perfect could be real. When Frank wants to be sweet, there's nobody like him.

I've traveled all over, in style. I mentioned France, Italy, Israel, but I've also been on safari in Africa, and watched bullfights in Spain (that was Alan's Hemingway period), and I've been entertained in the most elegant manner, because people wanted Alan around. He's funny, he's outgoing, he's warm, interesting, and people love to be with him.

You can't imagine the things I've done, things I could never have done had I not been married to Alan. It was truly a great ride, and none of it did I take seriously. I never lost sight of what I was and where I was. It was all fantasy, stuff you do, but later, you come home.

Which wasn't bad either. This house we live in has been great. We've had wonderful times here, wonderful dinner parties, wonderful birthday parties. In our tennis-crazed years, the courts were always filled, and we would play tennis and Alan would cook, and we had great help—a couple and a houseman—to see that everything ran smoothly.

Our life has changed. Now, Alan and I are together constantly; it's him and me. We play golf all year long (we have a house in Florida), and though we still see a lot of friends, we don't entertain so much at home, we eat in restaurants almost every night.

Four years ago, when he was operated on for cancer of the jaw, I was petrified. I couldn't believe it could happen to him. I've always been dependent on his strength, and to have him sick was very frightening.

As well as unexpected. Always it had been, "Oh, Alan can eat anything, Alan can drink anything, he can drink till all hours of the night, and in the morning he doesn't even need an aspirin." If I have a second drink, I'm sick, you have to put me in a shower to straighten me out. I couldn't drink *water* the way he drinks liquor. He was indestructible. Everybody said that.

Well, he proved he was not indestructible, and it scared me. I don't want anything to happen to him because I don't want to be without him. We've had some heartaches, like everybody else, but our life has been a lot of fun, and I don't want it to end.

I'm Mrs. Alan King, and I love it.

19 ↝ AU REVOIR

> *but wotthehell archy wotthehell*
> *jamais triste archy jamais triste*
> *that is my motto.*
> —DON MARQUIS

IF YOU'RE NOT familiar with *archy and mehitabel*, then you don't know it's written in lower case because archy the cockroach (its reputed author) couldn't manage the capital letters on the typewriter. And though archy's friend, mehitabel the cat, has seen better days— "What in hell have I done to deserve all these kittens?" she complains—she still urges herself to keep on trucking.

Take the song of mehitabel, which goes, in part:

> *oh i should worry and fret*
> *death and i will coquette*
> *there's a dance in the old dame yet*
> *toujours gai toujours gai.*

And you thought I was illiterate.

Anyhow, mehitabel the cat understood that it's the singing and the dancing that matter. And I've been singing and dancing all my life.

Most people start preparing for the future—for their grown-up years—by focusing. If you want to be a doctor, a dentist, a lawyer, you have to study hard. But I made a choice as a child that I was going to live by my wits, and show business is just about the only business where you don't have to pass a test, or get a license. (Every time they arrest a hooker and ask her occupation, she's either a model or an actress.)

The good thing about writing this book is I'll never have to tell these stories anymore, and Jeanette is pleased that she won't have to hear them anymore. Because, hopefully, the minute I open my mouth, someone is going to say, "I read that in your book."

But, I must confess, I'm tired. And what I'm tired of is all the bullshit. I grew up in an age of political giants; since then, things have changed, not always for the better. Now everything is politically correct, and the new politicians are not offering any new ideas, it's just rhetoric, it's like vocalizing. (I was never able to tell if a singer was good just by hearing him vocalize; vocal exercises are nothing but noises. And these days we're listening to noises, not ideas. We're looking at reflections in water.)

I've watched today's giants—the ones in my business—grow up. These young men are talented, but they seem to want it all. And the older ones can't get enough either. Show business has become *big* business. One guy is paid nineteen billion dollars, another guy is paid seventeen billion dollars, and all I'm hoping is that Grossinger's will reopen in my lifetime.

People are always asking me, "How much money do you have?" I say, "Not as much as you think, but more than I ever dreamed of. I have enough to be comfortable till the end of my days. That's if I drop dead Friday." (Old joke.)

Several times, I've been almost broke. As a young man I gambled; as an aging fool, I made a few bad investments, and didn't choose some of my partners wisely. Through it all, I paid my bills, lived high on the hog, and never—even when I was broke—gave up my car and chauffeur. That was not a convenience, it was a civic responsibility.

What would I do if I had my life to live over? The same things I've done, only I'd do them better. I would be a better husband, a better father, a better friend. I wouldn't drink, I wouldn't gamble, and I probably wouldn't be asked to write my memoirs.

I know I haven't given much space in these pages to my children. I respect—and want to protect—their privacy. Besides, my children aren't funny. Maybe they didn't suffer enough deprivation. Because in one way or another, comedy is a response to adversity. Most comedians have gone through some form of hardship in their early lives. Whether it was physical abuse, or poverty, or being an only child, or being a kid in a family so large you *wished* you were an only child, something goaded us into the spotlight.

For fifty years, my audiences have been loyal, and I'm grateful. When I talk about the pains of growing old, they totally identify. We grew old together.

Though some of the pains have come as a surprise to me. Four years ago, when I found out I had cancer of the jaw, I wasn't scared; I was stunned. I reacted as though I were having an out-of-body experience.

For seven weeks, my jaw was wired shut. For seven weeks, I was supposed to remain silent. Can you imagine me not being able to talk for seven weeks? When I was a kid, I'd learned ventriloquism, and now I discovered I could make myself understood even through my wired mouth. My surgeon called one day, and I answered the phone. He said, "May I speak to Alan King?" and I said, "Doc, I got news for you. You *are* speaking to Alan King." He said, "Why, that's remarkable." I said, "You think that's remarkable? I'm talking to you while drinking a glass of water."

When I was in the hospital, I received telegrams, letters, notes from all over the world, but the one that tickled me the most was from Sinatra. "Schmuck," it said, "give up smoking, and stick to hard candy." Look who's giving me advice—a man who's lived his life like a kamikaze pilot.

Obviously, my life has been a lot less colorful than Frank's (I'd like my wife to believe that), but I've had a lot of experiences. Though I still don't know if they've made me any smarter. My father used to say wisdom had nothing to do with age. "There's nothing says you gotta get smarter as you get older. I know a lot of dumb young men who turned into a lot of dumb old men."

These days, everybody keeps telling me I should slow down and smell the roses. Believe me, I've smelled the roses, and it's nowhere near as pleasurable as getting laughs. You only live once (except Shirley MacLaine), but if you work it right, once is enough. You gotta grab life by the balls, and hang on for the ride.

I'm hanging on. I still have eight-by-ten glossies, Max Factor #10, a pressed tuxedo, pierced ears, and will travel. So if there's anybody out there who has a bar mitzvah coming up, or a deli opening, or a gathering of any kind with more than twenty people, give me a call.

Finally, to paraphrase Joe E. Lewis, I hope you've had as much fun reading my life as I've had living it.

Index

Index

Made in the USA
Columbia, SC
19 October 2020